BIG

BOY

ZACH NEUHAUS

Author's Note:

I have changed the names of most people mentioned in this memoir. In some cases, I have altered physical descriptions and other identifying details.

I recognize that human memory is flawed and that others might recall things differently.

For all future developments, you can follow me on Instagram: zachneuhaus.

Acknowledgments

This memoir would not have been possible without the guidance of my therapist, Thom Smith, and my editor, Michael Mohr (https://www.michaelmohrwriter.com/).

I am also indebted to my friends and family. Your support has helped me through the most difficult parts of my life. Thank you all.

CONTENTS

1

Car Keys

Location: Kent, WA (South of Seattle)
Age: 6

The splash of water. A child's laughter. It was my laughter. Two birds chirped from the powerlines above the adjacent street, as cars buzzed by below. It was summer and the community pool at Papa's apartment was all mine. Mine and Uncle Bobby's.

Papa didn't come to the pool anymore, opting to stay inside, smoke, and watch baseball. He sent me out with his friend, who I was told to call my uncle, to play in the pool for an hour or two and then return to him. My little sister, Sarah, didn't come to the pool today and hadn't for the past few weeks. She didn't come to Papa's at all after nearly drowning a month ago.

Uncle Bobby had a dark mustache, dark eyebrows, and wispy, greying hair that was usually in a combover, but was a mess now in the water. He was in his 50s, I think, but frolicked around like a child that never grew up. And he had a farmer's tan, despite our weekly trips to the pool.

I climbed out of the water and walked quickly—dripping—to the ledge over the deep end, the pebble surface stinging my water-logged feet. Uncle Bobby pretended not to see me, looking away, towards one of the tables with a parasol. He was always easy to sneak up on.

Sensing the moment was right, I began my surprise attack, leaping towards him, my knees clutched to my chest. The water impacted my ears as I entered and sank to the bottom, coolness all around me, a welcome reprieve from the hot sun beating down on us. Well, it was hot for Kent, Washington anyways. My feet made impact with the scratchy white floor of the pool and I launched myself back to the surface, to continue my attack.

I found him as I always did, surprised and feigning fear at the onslaught I had unleashed. I shoved my hands through the water and splashed him mercilessly as he cried out in horror. "Ahhhh!" Then, just as predictably, he attempted to end the attack with one wide stroke of his arm, sending a tidal wave my way. I was prepared for that. I gulped air and ducked beneath the surface, then came back up to continue. The next wave hit me in the face right as I opened my mouth for air. I gagged and coughed, the sting of chlorine in my nostrils strong, and it was all over.

Uncle Bobby approached in the water and took hold of me, one hand on my chest and the other on my rear, holding it firmly. "You're alright. You really got me good there, Zach," he chuckled. He held me as I finished coughing. The birds chirped encouragement from the powerline.

Uncle Bobby glanced around for a moment, then whispered, "You wanna practice your Randy Savage elbow drops?"

I smiled and nodded enthusiastically. I loved watching wrestling and the pool was the perfect place to practice my moves. It wasn't allowed when I was with Papa or Mom though. They had both banned wrestling at the pool after I tried to suplex Sarah into the deep end. They weren't cool like Uncle Bobby. Grabbing hold of the railing, I walked up the steps, ready to impersonate the Macho Man in another leap from the ledge.

"Are you going to attack me again?" Uncle Bobby said in a faux sad tone. He whimpered and sniffled, looking down into the water, dejected.

"Noooooooo," I giggled.

"No come on, let's do it together. Come here," he beckoned, hands waving back towards himself.

I re-entered the pool and doggy paddled over to him. There was no longer any chirping from the birds. Their powerline perch was now vacant.

"Come around behind me and climb on my shoulders. Here give me your hand," he said as I paddled. He clutched each of my hands and raised me nearly out of the water. I lodged my feet against his shoulder blades and struggled to the top, my toenails scratching him as I went. He turned his head to the side but didn't complain. Once atop, my legs shook as I tried to balance myself.

"Straighten up. I'll hold your legs," he said as he released my hands, then moved his palms down to my thighs, accidentally lowering my shorts a bit. I stood up on his shoulders, his hands holding me in place. He walked forward.

"Where are we going?" I asked down to him.

"We need to be far from the walls, in case you lose your balance. That way you won't get hurt." I felt safe.

"Okay. Now you remember how he does it?" Uncle Bobby asked.

"OH YEEEEEAAAAH!" I mimicked, my eyes wide, glancing around like a man on the edge of sanity.

Uncle Bobby loosened his grip and said "Go!" and I jumped. My shorts got caught as I leapt, to the side with my elbow bent, aiming for the hapless wrestler in the water below. The cool water was a bit different on my rear, a telltale sign I'd been exposed. I pulled up my shorts under the water, then swam to the top and opened my eyes just in time to see Uncle Bobby resurface. I was confused about why he went under water but didn't mention it.

"That wasn't very good," I said, "I thought you let go?"

"We just need to practice to get it right," Uncle Bobby wiped his eyes. "Come here."

We tried a few more times, and each time my shorts got caught on something as I took flight. I no longer cared about the inconvenience. It was just nice to feel like a kid again, to have someone pay attention to me and have fun. Papa didn't talk much after the divorce. Mom was already dating someone new. I didn't have many friends and Sarah didn't even come on our visits anymore. Uncle Bobby came along and became my friend at just the right time. I kind of stole him from Papa and he always spent way more time with me than with the old man. As I resurfaced for the fifth time, I was overcome by an emotion I hadn't experienced in a while: gratitude. I hugged him.

"How about the Hulkster?" Uncle Bobby asked, "You think you can do his leg drop?"

"Yeah I can!" I liked Hulk Hogan, too.

"I don't know. He's pretty cool. Sure, you can do it, BROTHER?" he tried to say the last part like Hogan did.

"I know I can!"

I paddled around behind him and climbed up as before, his hands helping me as I went.

"Okay. You ready, BROTHER?" I called down to him. Uncle Bobby laughed and then laughed harder, his head tilted up, eyes looking up my legs. I waited.

The laughter caused his right shoulder to heave, which threw me off balance, and I fell. A moment of panic was calmed as his hands grabbed my hips and slowly guided me down to the water. I brushed against him all the way down and there was something hard in his shorts. I didn't know what it was, but assumed it was car keys or something.

"You gotta be careful, kid," he said, now hugging me from behind, the car keys pressed against me.

"I know. I'm sorry."

"It's alright. Probably time for us to get going anyways. Let's go dry off." He let go of me, I paddled away to the stairs, and we walked to the men's room after grabbing our clothes from the table with the parasol.

Inside, I was confronted with the problem I always have in public pool restrooms. *Is the floor wet because people have been drying off? Or is it wet because someone has peed on it?* The faint aroma of chlorine combined with the smell of unwashed toilet led me to conclude it might be a bit of both. I was disgusted but also had no shoes or sandals.

Uncle Bobby stood in the doorway, observing, as I dropped a towel to the floor to mitigate my disgust. I stood on it, then removed my shorts and began drying off with a second towel. Uncle Bobby walked towards me and as I looked up, I could see him looking at me, but not at my face. His gaze was much lower.

"Uncle Bobby?" I murmured. He looked up at my face, then darted into a bathroom stall. I resumed toweling myself off.

A slapping sound began emanating from the stall. Slow at first, it gained speed and then suddenly stopped. There was the sound of toilet paper being pulled hastily from a roll on a rickety rod, a slight squeak. I leaned against the wall, now dressed and dry enough for the journey home.

The toilet flushed, and he emerged from the stall, a blank stare on his face. Uncle Bobby didn't dry off or comb his mussed hair or even put his shirt on. He grabbed my hand without looking at me, and we began walking home.

We exited the bathroom and walked along the pebble path, past the rental office adjoining the bathrooms, up the steps, and out onto the black paved parking lot and the road back to Papa's.

Uncle Bobby and I usually jogged back after swimming. We always forgot shoes and the black pavement was hot in the summer. Unbearable when you're six years old. No jogging today, though I tried. I leapt forward onto the black pavement and attempted to run, but his hand was firmly locked on mine and his pace didn't vary. I stumbled back, then looked up at him. His face was as before, blank, eyes unblinking, looking dead ahead. Confused, I acquiesced to his pace and hopped on alternating feet to alleviate the painful, hot pavement.

We approached Papa's apartment and Uncle Bobby released my hand. I took off for the little concrete steps and the path that led to the front door. The path was in the shade, between patches of grass, cool on my damaged feet. A car door opened and closed, and I turned around just in time to see Uncle Bobby back out and leave, faster than would seem appropriate for a residential area. Not a word was exchanged in his parting that day.

Did I do something wrong?

2

Mario and Luigi

Location: Maple Valley, WA (Southeast of Seattle)
Age: 5

My mother was born in Seattle in the 1950s. Her friends called her Deb or Debby. Her mother, my Nana, was a devout Christian woman who grew up on a dairy farm in Oconomowoc, Wisconsin. That dairy farm upbringing instilled in Nana a solid work ethic, which came in handy when her husband walked out the door and left her with a child to raise on her own.

Mom never referred to her father as her father, simply calling him Al instead. I never met him, though our lives did overlap some. Mom gave me the opportunity to meet him once, when word reached her that Al was on his deathbed. I declined. At that point, I knew the stories and reasons why Mom didn't like him. Among them, he used to beat her for all sorts of things, like not finishing her vegetables. Since he ran out on them, Nana had to work... a lot. Mom didn't see her much. Bad grades and fights at school naturally followed. Nana tried to introduce new father figures to

7

Mom's life, but they didn't last, and one of them molested her. Her childhood was a sad one for the most part. But, it turns out, Mom was very pretty, and she became a professional model for several years in her late teens and early twenties. It was her way out.

My father, who I always called Papa, was born in Illinois in the 1920s. His friends called him Frosty. I don't know why. He grew up during the Great Depression, losing both of his parents during that time. He dropped out of high school and moved to Texas to live with his stepbrother. That stepbrother was a crop duster and Papa would later recall that the first time he went flying with him, was the moment he realized that the only thing he wanted to do in life was be a pilot. He enlisted in the U.S. Army in 1944 and was on active duty until 1946. The G.I. Bill got him a private pilot's license, which got him a shot at becoming an officer in the newly created United States Air Force. He served for 20 years in total and parlayed that experience into a job as an airline pilot in Hawaii.

In Hawaii, Papa met a former-model-turned-flight-attendant 30 years younger than him. They got married in Reno and they birthed me and my little sister, Sarah. Eventually, Papa lost his wings due to age, and worked various contracts overseas and non-flying jobs closer to home, before resigning himself to living off his military pension and social security.

We lived in a small house in Kent, Washington for my first few years. After Sarah arrived, the house was no longer large enough, so we moved a half hour away, to Maple Valley, where I spent the rest of my childhood. Our house there was baby blue with white trim in a new neighborhood with a few trees in the backyard.

***

Everything was going well, until it suddenly wasn't. Isn't that always the case when you're a kid? As a child, only five at the time, I didn't see it coming.

The day started much the same as any other. I woke up and went downstairs to eat, wearing gray sweatpants and a blue, Yale University sweatshirt. My parents thought I was smart, so a place like Yale was where I was supposed to go. Mom gave me a bowl of Fruit Loops, a side of sliced bananas, and a glass of orange juice. My standard breakfast. I sat down at the table with my sister seated on the other side. Sarah had unkempt light brown hair and pink overalls on. She sat on her knees in the chair since she wasn't tall enough to get over the table otherwise.

Papa came down the stairs shortly after, fully dressed in white polo and gray slacks. When he got to the bottom of the stairs he paused, took out a white handkerchief and rubbed his big glasses with it. He put his glasses back on, then looked at Mom for a moment, blinking a few times through the lenses. It was a look of stunned recognition, of what, I didn't know at the time. He resumed walking, down the second, smaller set of stairs, to the bottom floor, and then out into the garage. Mom said, "put your dishes in the sink when you're done," as she followed him out, wearing only a white bathrobe, her brown hair flowing behind her. The door to the garage was heavier than a normal door and it slammed like always. Sarah and I looked at each other across the table, her mouth already full of food. I stuck my tongue out at her, and she frowned with an "hmph" noise, then I grinned and started eating.

I made quick work of the Fruit Loops, even though I knew I should start with the bananas. They get brown if you wait. The television was on behind me, but I stared out the kitchen windows instead. Gray skies. There was a pitter-patter of rain on the roof and streaks of water rushed down the window glass. I liked the rain. It meant I could stay inside and staying inside meant I could probably play Nintendo, which was by far my favorite thing. Mom only let me play for a half hour, but on rainy days she sometimes let me go over that. Other times I just cheated and reset the egg timer when she wasn't looking. I could usually stretch to at least an hour, maybe longer.

The garage door opened just as I was dropping my dishes off in the sink. I used my spoon to covertly brush the disgusting banana slices into the garbage disposal, then turned around to see Papa walk up the small flight of stairs. I smiled and tried to meet his gaze, but he looked down at the steps instead, then down at the floor, then down at the steps again as he ascended the same staircase he had descended from just moments ago. Mom followed him upstairs to their bedroom, offering me a brief, nervous smile while in transit, then averting her gaze as well.

Is Papa mad at me? He doesn't like how much I play video games, always telling me to "go outside and enjoy it before you're old like me and can't."

"Hey Mom!" I yelled up the stairs.

"Yes, Zach?" Mom replied.

"Can I go outside and ride my bike?" *Maybe Papa will be pleased by this.*

"Sure. Make sure you wear a jacket and put on your helmet."

I walked from the staircase towards the front door. A gentle tug on my hand startled me and I turned around. It was Sarah. "No, Ya Ya," she said, looking up at me, her light brown hair unkempt, the remains of some food smeared by the right corner of her mouth. Sad eyes. She called me "Ya Ya" because "Zach" is too hard for a two-year-old.

"I'll be back later, Sarah," I reassured her. "Let go." I pulled my hand away.

Sarah made another "hmph" noise with a frown, then took a few steps back, sad eyes still locked on me. I put on my jacket and shoes, then walked outside, over to the side yard where my bike was. My white helmet was wet, as was the seat of the Huffy. As I wiped them off with the sleeve of my sweatshirt, I mentally prepared my strategy.

I'll ride my bike around the neighborhood four times. That will take a while and I'll be soaked when I get home. Mom will make me change and if I sniffle some she will make me stay inside. Papa will be pleased that I played outside. They will let me play Nintendo.

I walked my bike down to the sidewalk, sat on it, and peddled away, confident that Mario and Luigi and I would be reunited soon.

***

The rain soaked me faster than I anticipated. I was drenched and genuinely sniffling by the time lap 4 was complete. Walking my bike back to the side yard, I noticed that Papa's car had gone missing.

Maybe he's running errands.

I took my shoes off outside, placing them next to the front door, as I'd been told to do when they're wet. Mom was waiting for me inside, standing next to the large staircase. She was still in her bathrobe. Her eyes were glassy and pink now, which made her pupils intense, especially while they were aimed at me. I had never seen her cry before, and she wasn't crying now, but I assumed she had been. Her eyes were like Sarah's when she was done crying. This made me feel anxious, and I didn't know what to do about it, so I just stood by the front door, letting time pass until she spoke.

"You're all wet," she finally remarked. I walked closer to her.

"Yeah. I wanted to play outside because Papa likes it when I do," I said sheepishly, looking at the floor, not wanting to face whatever had happened.

"Go upstairs and put on your Ninja Turtle pajamas. You don't need to go outside anymore today."

Success!

I did as I was told, then returned downstairs, and made a beeline for the television and my beloved Mario and Luigi. I sat on the beige carpet and pressed the button to turn on the Nintendo. Mom sat on the couch behind me just as the red curtain was raising on *Mario Bros 3*.

"Zach," came a timid voice from behind me. I hesitated, then tilted my head towards her.

"Zach… we need to talk. Come here." I sat on the couch next to her.

Mom put her arm over my shoulder, holding me against her, then turned my world upside-down. "Your father and I don't love each other anymore. He won't be living here from now on. I want you to know tha…" I ran from her to the bathroom next to the garage, closing the door quickly behind me, pressing the button on the knob until it clicked, locking her out.

I stood in the bathroom for a moment, then heard soft footsteps approach the door, and a stiff wiggle of the locked doorknob. "Zach," Mom pleaded from the other side. "Please come out."

I didn't answer her. I turned the lights off and pressed my back against the door, sliding down it until my butt rested on the cold tiled floor. My hair was still wet from the bike ride, my sniffling was from the cold I felt on the outside and now inside as well. I could tell I was crying because the water dribbling down my face was warm. Sitting there in the cold, dark bathroom, I ignored Mom's repeated pleas for me to return to her. Little Sarah came by and knocked and said "Ya Ya, what?" I ignored her, too, shaking my head back and forth in silent agony for the rest of the day.

3

Big Boys Don't Cry

Location: Kent, WA
Age: 6

Papa's apartment was nothing to boast of and he lived alone. Most days when I went over, he would post up in his bedroom watching baseball or golf, drinking, and smoking Winston Light 100s until the room filled with smoke. He was a fat old man, bald except for a brown ring of hair, with large glasses, a mustache, and always in sweatpants. Upon closer inspection, one could see faint pock marks mixed in with his wrinkly face, remnants of a boyhood spent during the Great Depression, when there was still acne but not creams to deal with it.

Papa didn't have a chair in his bedroom, so he sat on the edge of his bed with a beechwood folding snack table in front of him, to lean on and stack the things he needed for the day. Ashtray, pack of smokes, and either a four-pack of single serving wine bottles or a pint of vodka, and a small cup. There was a towel to sit on so that he wouldn't leave streaks on the mattress and his slippers sat next to the bed. He never wore socks as he couldn't reach his feet easily, if at all, and his toenails grew longer than seemed appropriate.

Papa was distant, but he always told me he loved me when he took me back to Mom's. Mom told me not to go in his room due to all the smoke and she admonished him whenever he smoked in the dirty blue van he drove. It was dirty on the inside but not outside. Papa had his military pension and social security. Money came in every month and went out every month and he had no problem driving up to a car wash to get it cleaned, though he never bothered with vacuuming or garbage.

I spent most of my visits roaming around his apartment, watching TV, and playing with my Legos. I practiced my wrestling moves on two old mattresses in the second bedroom, which functioned as our playroom. Occasionally, I'd sit on this old brown couch, with blue and pink stains from Gak and silly putty stuck in the fabric, in the living room and read *Put me in the Zoo* to Sarah, her little feet dangling over the turquoise carpet below.

A few months after the divorce a friend of my fathers started to come by the apartment. He brought Butterfinger candy bars and toy guns. He would help me build my Lego castles in the playroom and asked me questions about what the king was doing and if he liked his knights or not. Papa told me to call his friend "Uncle Bobby." At first, I assumed he actually was my uncle, but Mom told me he was not.

Uncle Bobby was a few years younger than Papa, I'd guess late 50s. He also had a mustache and a bit of a belly, but less pronounced than Papa's. He compensated for his balding hair by arranging a thin combover. He didn't have glasses, except while reading, and dressed better than Papa, though nothing too fancy. Whenever he came over, he would briefly chat with Papa, who would then retire to his bedroom, leaving Sarah and I in Bobby's

14

care. I initially had an uncertain feeling about him and his interest in playing with me; it seemed unusual. I wondered why he never came by when Mom and Papa were together, but assumed I was just too young to remember it.

***

Spring arrived and the small pool at Papa's apartment community opened for the season. I would go to the pool with Papa and Uncle Bobby every time I visited. Papa liked to pretend he was a whale, slowly diving under and resurfacing with high-pitched "meeeee" sounds, and Uncle Bobby would let me stand on his shoulders and jump off.

There were seldom other people there in springtime, but that changed in the summer. Papa changed too. He didn't like going to the pool when there were a lot of people, so I just went with Uncle Bobby. I asked him why Papa wouldn't come anymore, and he said my old man had a problem about his body like Marlon Brando in *Apocalypse Now*. That childhood reference is what caused me to initially watch that movie, so I guess my association with Uncle Bobby wasn't a total loss.

After the incident at the pool, Uncle Bobby didn't come to Papa's for a while. I assumed it was because of me, but Papa told me Bobby had to get surgery for something, I don't remember what. It was a few days after the 4th of July that I saw him again. He came in with the usual Butterfingers and brought bratwurst for Papa to grill out back on his tiny patio.

Papa liked to barbecue bratwurst or steaks. It was basically all he knew how to cook. The rest of the time, we just ate out at *Azteca* or this Chinese place named *Eng's* in Kent, which is now closed. *Eng's* was also Papa's regular place to drink at when he went out. He liked it because even though it was Chinese, it had a German bartender. "She's got some nice breasts," he used to say.

15

While Papa was out grilling, Uncle Bobby sat down on the couch next to me. His face was clammy and his usual thin combover was tussled like he'd just walked in from the wind.

"Did your Papa tell you I had surgery?" He asked.

"Yeah."

"Wanna see my scar?"

I was curious about that. I fell about a year prior and had a scar on my knee. It was interesting to me that sometimes the body doesn't heal all the way. Uncle Bobby stood up and gestured to follow him, so like a lamb to the slaughter, I did. The next thing I know, we're in the bathroom adjoining the playroom, and Uncle Bobby is undoing his belt and lowering his pants. I remember feeling startled and like something was wrong and not knowing what to do. The truth is I froze. Uncle Bobby had a scar on his pelvis, a bright pink one.

"You see what they did to Uncle Bobby?"

I said nothing.

"You love me like I'm your real uncle, right?"

I nodded.

"Why don't you kiss my boo boo and make it better?"

I didn't. I started to cry instead, tears running down my face. Uncle Bobby wiped my tears away and told me "I thought you were a big boy? Be a big boy now. Big boys don't cry." Then he took my hand and put it on his penis. He said he loved me like I was his "real nephew." Then he unzipped my pants, lowered them, and reached in my underwear. My memory becomes fuzzy at this point. I don't know how long it went on, but by the end I could smell bratwurst. Papa had brought some in on a plate and gone out to cook more. He always cooked more than necessary, so he had something quick to eat the next day. He was lazy like that.

Upon smelling the brats, I peered up and saw a sweaty mustache with intense eyes staring down at me. I looked away, to the off-white wall, then the faded pink and green floral pattern on

16

the unwashed, tiled floor. My hand was moving, but I didn't dare look at it, and what it was doing. Eventually, I heard the heavy breathing of an old man. The labored breaths became louder and then he spun around to face the shower and I heard slapping sounds again. Sensing an opening, my mind shifted to escaping. I turned to run but forgot my pants were down, causing me to barrel face and shoulder first into the door.

It must have made a good amount of noise, because Papa opened the sliding door and hollered, "Everything alright in there?"

Uncle Bobby made his escape through the second bathroom door, making his way into the playroom, then through another door to the other side of the bathroom door I smacked into. He knocked on the door. "You okay in there, Zach?"

I didn't answer.

"Zach? You alright?" He asked again. His tone was anxious. The doorknob began shaking above me.

"Zach?"

"I'm okay," I replied, but I didn't feel like it.

***

One of my first memories was eating bratwurst and potatoes with Papa. This was before the divorce. Papa explained to me where our family name came from and how his father served in the U.S. Army during World War I even though his name was Adolph. "We weren't 'bad Germans,'" the old man explained, using his hands to make air quotes. I felt close to Papa when he told me stories and the brats were delicious. After Uncle Bobby, I couldn't eat bratwurst until I was nearly 30 and drunk with some friends at *Shultzy's* in Seattle.

4

Where my sense of humor comes from

Location: Kent, WA
Age: 6

What more can I say about my father? He was a creature of habit. One of his favorite habits was the daily trip to *Eng's*. He went there every evening that he wasn't visited by Sarah and me. Sometimes he took us there also.

The four of us – Papa, Uncle Bobby, Sarah, and I – got out of the blue van and walked to the entrance of *Eng's*. Stepping inside we were greeted by a smiling woman who recognized my father immediately.

"Oh, hello Frosty. How are you?" She greeted. She walked from behind a counter, her arm raised to the side, pointing to her left, towards the bar. Then, noticing the two children in tow, she lowered her arm and said "Oh. Would you like a table today?"

"Yes, please. A booth." Papa replied. The restaurant was devoid of customers. It was not a question of getting a booth or not. Rather, which booth did we want?

We walked past a tank full of pet fish. *Glub, glub, glub,* their mouths went while we passed. *Cute.* The restaurant was cooler than outside, but not overly so. The lighting was a bit lower, too. I always felt relaxed when we came to *Eng's* for dinner. We'd been there several times before with Papa and Uncle Bobby. Things were different now though.

We ascended two steps to the dining area, a maroon carpet forming the path, with tables and wooden chairs on the right, and six booths on the left lining the wall. The booths were maroon also, with rubber-like seats that compressed slightly beneath your butt, and fabric backrests. Half-oval, with the table in the middle, small cream-colored cups for tea on each paper placemat. There were large mirrors along the left wall, spaced evenly to line up with each booth, stretching at least six feet in height. A solitary, dim wall light filled the gap between each of these giant mirrors. A bottle of soy sauce sat on each table.

Papa made his selection, and we sat down for dinner. Sarah and I slid to the inside of the oval, with Papa and Uncle Bobby sitting at the exits. The host smiled pleasantly then placed our menus in front of us and departed.

We knew what we were going to eat. It was almost always the same. Sometimes Sarah and I would agitate for a new menu item, and sometimes Papa would grant such a request, but not today. Sarah and I didn't even look at the menu this time. The best dish we ate was the plate of sliced pork with hot mustard and sesame seeds. That was my favorite. There were chicken and noodle dishes too, but the main event was the sliced pork and the mustard that hurt me the first time, but that I eventually came to love. Uncle Bobby, bifocals on, still went through the motions of checking the menu as we waited for the waitress to come over.

"I gotta take a leak," Papa said, butt-sliding to exit the booth and walking down two small steps to the men's room. He was in his customary green sweatpants and white polo shirt.

A woman approached him before he entered the restroom. There was a sound of hollering as they greeted each other, but I couldn't make out what was said. They hugged, and Papa said a few more things, glancing over at us and gesturing with his right hand as if to say, "I'm here with the kids tonight." The woman smiled at us and waved. I gave a half-hearted wave back. Papa disappeared into the bathroom.

"Who was that?" I wondered out loud.

"The one by your Papa?" Uncle Bobby asked, eyes still down on the menu.

"Yeah. Does she work here?"

"She's the bartender. Frosty's favorite. Only white gal in the place."

"Why is she the only one?"

"Ha ha. Why do you think?" Uncle Bobby stared down at me with inquisition in his eyes. I didn't know what to say, so I said nothing. He made a disapproving "hmph" noise and then resumed scanning the menu.

A smiling girl approached the table, notepad in hand.

"Hello. Are you ready to order?" Her tone was pleasant, warm. She was a teenager, but her voice didn't sound grown up yet. I thought she was beautiful. And I stared.

Uncle Bobby smiled at her, then glanced over at me, noticing my interest. He placed his hand on my thigh, under the table, and said, "Why don't you tell the nice Ori*ntal gal what we're having?" Sarah thought Uncle Bobby was teasing me about liking the waitress. Her little giggles punctuated the silence that followed.

The waitress lowered her eyes, her smile vanishing right when Uncle Bobby had said "Ori*ntal." Then, as if reminding herself of her duties, she looked back up, smiling at me, pen and pad in hand.

"Please. Pork slices," I managed to say. She nodded and wrote it on the pad, then raised her eyebrows expectantly.

"And?" Uncle Bobby asked, inquisition in his eyes again. His hand migrated up my thigh and his pinky finger started slowly prodding my genitals. I gasped, and my legs trembled. I could no longer speak.

"Okay then," Uncle Bobby remarked. He talked to the waitress, his hand now clutching my crotch beneath the table. I don't remember what he said to her, but she wrote some more things down and then walked away.

Uncle Bobby rubbed his fingers up and down on my crotch. My legs were still trembling, and my right leg bumped his. That knowledge encouraged him, as he smiled and began rubbing more vigorously. He was covert about it, moving only his hand, concealed beneath the table, rather than his whole arm. He bit his lower lip, eyeing me, and I lowered my head and looked away.

Papa exited the men's room, shaking his hands to dry them. I thought I might be saved. He approached our table, then held up one finger as if to say, "one minute," and waddled down to the bar. It was to be one of the longest minutes of my life.

"Ha ha. Your Papa sure does like that gal," Uncle Bobby said. An eternity passed under the table.

I tried to distract myself by watching the people who had just been seated at the table in front of us. Two red-haired adults. One man and one woman. Both the lighter side of pale and with similar, pointed noses. They were smiling at each other and talking in friendly tones. *Maybe they're brother and sister and haven't seen each other in a long time.* Their hands were all above the table. The man leaned in and, smiling, said something to the woman. She leaned back and laughed, then said, a bit too loudly, "Oh, you ass!" and wiped her left eye while continuing to laugh. The man chuckled a bit to himself, satisfied. I was glancing into another world. And that's what hurt the most, knowing that something else was possible, that I was just unlucky. That for whatever reason, this was my lot in life.

My legs trembling, breathing becoming tight, I tilted my head up just enough to see Uncle Bobby digging his teeth into his lower lip, determined. Elbows on the table, I rested my chin on my hands and tried to focus on the redheads and their wonderful life.

"I need to go potty," Sarah finally said. I looked her way and greeted her as a liberator, with a smile.

"Oh, alright. Let's go," Uncle Bobby said. He released my genitals while butt-sliding out of the booth. Sarah slid forward off the seat, under the table, and crawled out, then followed him to the restroom. I was sad that Sarah was now alone with him, but also relieved to have my privates back.

I sat there, trembling, for a few moments. The pretty girl walked by and glanced at me, and I glanced back, and neither of us said anything. Papa emerged from the bar area, glass in hand, and slowly waddled back to our table.

"Where'd everyone go?" he asked as he slid back into the booth.

"Sarah needed to pee," I replied.

Papa took a sip from his glass, swallowed, then exhaled with satisfaction. Clear liquid, but I knew it wasn't water. He looked at me, then towards the men's room as Sarah and Uncle Bobby walked out.

Our food arrived moments later, and I ate until my stomach hurt. And then I kept eating. The redheads sipped tea and continued to chat.

We passed by the fish tank on the way out. I pondered them in that tank and believed that they were sad to be in there, trapped. *Trapped like me, though no one seems to be hurting them in their cage. Then again, people don't always notice bad things being done. I'm sorry, fish.* The fish *glub glubbed* at me and I raised my hand to touch their glass. They swam to the other side of the tank and didn't look back.

Papa opened the door and led us outside to the parking lot. It was very dark out now. Without warning, an evil, raucous noise bellowed from Papa's sweatpants, as I was walking directly behind him.

"Heh heh heh," Papa chuckled, head turned to the side, smiling with yellowed, misshapen teeth, one eye looking back at us.

I resigned myself to the onslaught rapidly approaching my face. It was putrid, but I was getting used to it. His entire apartment smelled like an aired-out version of it anyways.

"Wooooo!" Uncle Bobby exclaimed, waving his hand in the air in a vain attempt to avoid the fumes. "Jesus, Frost."

Papa kept laughing, looking back at us. I started laughing too. It was better than crying.

We got in the blue van that was dirty on the inside and clean on the outside and drove back to the apartment.

5

Thanksgiving

Location: Kent & Maple Valley, WA
Age: 6

I never played sick to get out of going to school, but I did fake it to avoid going to Papa's. I remember feeling like I would get in trouble if anyone found out about what Uncle Bobby did, like it was my fault or something. It happened almost every time I went over there now. I didn't want to tell my parents. It was Papa's friend after all; I figured he would be mad at me, which might make him spend less time with me than he already did. Mom was dating a smarmy tyrant who would later become my stepfather. She had other things on her mind and after the way she hurt me with the divorce, I had no reason to not believe she wouldn't hurt me again. The divorce had been her idea.

I started to have nightmares about being put up for adoption or being taken away by the police. As shitty as my life seemed at the time, I thought it could get a whole lot worse. Mom became

24

suspicious of my being sick every time Papa's visitation was scheduled, so she started making me go anyways. I knew I had to be clever to get away from Uncle Bobby.

Papa owned a gun, a revolver, and I had a general idea of where he kept it. After a particularly bad session with Uncle Bobby, I went to Papa's bedroom, braving the smoke and thin film of dust on everything, to search for a solution to my problem. Sarah hadn't come to visit that day because she had a doctor's appointment. Uncle Bobby and Papa were out on the patio, drinking and bullshitting, staring out at gray fence six feet of grass away, the full extent of the backyard, with cars passing on the other side. I climbed up the shelves in Papa's closet and finally got to the top.

The revolver had been passed around a bit. Papa bought it for Mom when she was pregnant with me. He had a job that involved traveling to Guam for months at a time back then. Mom was always vague about what that job entailed, but my last surviving aunt tells me he was contracted by the government. Papa always refused to talk about it. Mom gave the gun back to him in the divorce, but he didn't accept that at first, so it sat at a lawyer's office, where he claimed it months later after a car down the street from his apartment was broken into. It had been sitting on the top shelf of his closet, next to his heavily dusted Air Force officer hat and wings. I grabbed the gun and descended, placing it on the next shelf down as I went.

I put the gun in my pants, which gave me a chill, and tiptoed as quickly as I could to the playroom. I closed the door and reoriented a pile of dirty clothes on the floor, so I would have a place to hide it if needed. I sat on an old, stained and yellowed stack of mattresses and pulled the gun out to inspect it. It was cold and slimy. It was heavier than I expected, and the weight was uneven. I placed it on the old red-and-gold Persian rug at my feet and looked at it for a while. Something seemed wrong about it. I had never held a real gun before but had a suspicion about this one. I got on all fours and leaned my face down to it. I inspected the barrel, then opened the cylinder. There were no bullets. *Dammit.*

I heard the sliding door open and knew my plan was foiled for now. I moved the pile of clothes to the corner and put the gun inside of it. Papa never went in the playroom anyways.

***

A few molestations later, I saw another opportunity and went to Papa's room to search for the bullets. We had Mexican food for dinner that night, Uncle Bobby had already left, and Papa was experiencing gastric distress. I heard him in the bathroom next to the closet. *Splash splash* and a groan, accompanied by an uneven, squeaking fan, as if it were dying from the smell too. I climbed the shelves and used a small flashlight to look on each one for bullets. I couldn't find any. *What type of person owns a gun but not any bullets?* I searched his nightstand and dresser and behind his TV. I held my breath and dropped to the floor to look under his bed. All I found down there was a spider who followed the light back towards me, so I ran. I gave up on the gun plan but never thought to move the gun from its hiding place in the playroom until Papa moved to a new apartment closer to us, many years later. He never noted its absence.

***

Papa had a Polaroid camera that we sometimes played with on birthdays or holidays. I thought it was neat to be able to take a picture and have it developed right in front of you. Uncle Bobby liked the camera too; he would take pictures of me when I was lounging on the couch in sweatpants or in Papa's blue robe. I wore Papa's robe whenever I was feeling cold after a swim and would splay out on the couch so there was no space for Uncle Bobby to sit near me. I noticed Uncle Bobby would take some of the photos with him when he left, leaving the others for us to have. I wondered about that, what those photos might be.

The day after Thanksgiving, I went over to Papa's apartment. Mom made plates of leftovers that Papa reheated and the four of us – Papa, Sarah, Uncle Bobby, me – sat down to eat. We got out the camera and later Uncle Bobby took pictures of me on the couch. I was laying on my side because my stomach was upset from so much food. Mom taught me to lay on my left side to assist with digestion.

Papa and Uncle Bobby had a few drinks out on the patio after that, by the grill. I saw my opportunity and I took it; I grabbed the stack of developed Polaroids and took them into the bathroom, locking the door behind me. There were multiple pictures of my sweatpants-covered ass, mixed in with the usual holiday photos of the food and smiles and all that. I was filled with dread. I took half the ass pictures and hid them in the bathroom, then put the photos back out where they had been.

Uncle Bobby did his usual thing where he would take a few of the photos home with him. Now I knew which ones he'd been taking. He scratched the side of his face, then furrowed his brow, while looking through the photos. I worried he might be on to me. He shrugged it off, said goodbye, and left with his photos. When it was time for Papa to drive Sarah and I home, I went to the bathroom and grabbed the hidden photos, then added them back to the stack and brought them with me. I told Papa I wanted to show Mom our Thanksgiving photos. He didn't care, which was no surprise at that point. He swerved us home.

When Sarah and I got dropped off with Mom, she asked how Thanksgiving was at Papa's. I told her we took some pictures and handed them to her. We sat down on the couch. She was drinking a gin and tonic. My soon-to-be stepfather was out in the garage listening to country music and moving tools around. Mom flipped through the photos and stopped when she got to the ass shots. She let out an uncomfortable laugh and asked Sarah "Did you take pictures of your brother's tush?" There was a shake of the head from her and Mom side-eyed me. *This is it. This is when I get put up for adoption.*

"Zach, when you go to Papa's, who uses the camera?"

"Oh, we all do, but mostly Uncle Bobby."

"Did Uncle Bobby use the camera tonight?"

"Yeah, I was laying on the couch cuz I was too full."

Mom started to freak out, shuffling through the pictures to find all the ass shots, saying "Oh my God." I leapt off the couch and ran upstairs to my bedroom. I closed the door and put my ear against it. She was interrogating Sarah now. I left her behind to save myself.

A few moments later, I heard Mom walk to the kitchen and pick up the phone and call Papa. Mom started yelling. Papa made things worse by being drunk on the other end, which made Mom yell even more because she figured he drove us home loaded. He did. I opened my door slowly, then crept halfway down the stairs and peaked over the railing to the kitchen where Mom was. She was shaking her gin and tonic for emphasis as she issued threats. "IF BOBBY IS AROUND THE KIDS AGAIN, WE ARE GOING BACK TO COURT!"

6

Latex

Location: Kent, WA
Age: 6

My faking illness to avoid Papa's had an unintended consequence: Mom became a hypochondriac on my behalf. It wasn't the first time. When I was very little, I "almost died" from giardia. Mom went round for round with military doctors, all of whom told her I was fine, but I kept losing weight and couldn't stop puking or shitting myself, so she went to a civilian doctor and got some medication. That cured me of the giardia and she wanted to sue the military, but Papa was a company man and wouldn't allow it. The maternal hypochondria abated by the time they got divorced, but it came back when I started faking sick to avoid Uncle Bobby.

Mom took me to the doctor anytime I got the sniffles. I liked this at first because it made me think she cared. After the Polaroid photo incident, Mom also began inspecting my body when I came back from Papa's. "Was Uncle Bobby there? Did you get hurt?" taking my clothes off, with urgency in her voice like I was poisoned, and she was looking for the antidote. It was during one of these inspections that she discovered part of my foreskin was attached to the head of my penis. She worried that it was abnormal. "Maybe they didn't cut it right," she said. Another appointment was scheduled.

We always went to the same doctor's office in Kent and the staff there knew Mom was the overly concerned type. This appointment had been scheduled right before Christmas, so my usual doctor was not there, and we had to go to the third floor. It was my first time on the third floor, and I worried they wouldn't have the activity cubes in the waiting room like on the second floor. They did and there weren't any other children there, so I had it all to myself. I stood next to the cube and played with the wire-and-bead maze toy on top while Mom sat down and read the newspaper. It always smelled terrible at the doctor's office, like it was clean and dirty at the same time. I imagined I was breathing in some sickness whenever we went.

I don't remember the doctor's name, but he was white and had a brown mustache and brown hair like my usual doctor. We went into one of the exam rooms and Mom explained the problem. I was instructed to drop my pants and he put on some latex gloves and lifted my penis and found the errant foreskin.

"It's what we call redundant skin. They left too much foreskin, and some has attached. Being a bit heavy also contributes."

"Will it still grow to be normal size?"

Wow Mom.

"Yeah that won't be an issue. When a skin bridge like this forms, the worry is more about discomfort or curvature."

"He's going to have a bent dick?"

I felt like I was dying.

"Not necessarily. We can always check on it when he hits puberty. If it's an issue, he will have some discomfort when he starts getting erections. It will feel like he's being tugged down during arousal."

"Is there anything we can do today?" Mom asked.

Mom and the doctor went back and forth for a few minutes, with her vicarious anxiety demanding a solution and the doctor's overworked expertise desiring to put things off. I observed earlier in life that to be a child meant being a hostage to adult games of emotional hot potato. You just have to sit there and hope the hot potato lands on the right adult so nothing bad happens. There's nothing else you can do. They don't give a damn about a child's opinion. The only times they even ask for a child's opinion is when they're hoping the child will regurgitate their adult opinions. And they're strongly disappointed when that's not the case. *What's the point?* I tuned them out while looking at a lung cancer poster hanging on the wall. Back then I didn't think lung cancer was real because Papa smoked a ton and never got it.

A decision was made, and the doctor got back on his knees in front of me. I looked at Mom as his hands took hold of my penis. She looked away, seemingly out the window, except the lavender blinds were closed. I peered down at the doctor and saw a mustache with latex fingers moving around in front of me. Three of the latex fingers gripped the tip of my penis. More fingers reached under the tip, to the side of it I couldn't see from above and clutched at a piece of skin. Then there was a pulling feeling. Dull pain. Dull pain with growing intensity. Then relief, as the doctor let go. *Maybe that was it.* But it wasn't. He adjusted his grip and began again. The pain was back. It continued to climb as the doctor pinched and pulled harder.

"Please no," I whimpered as I took half a step back. The doctor leaned forward, maintaining his hold.

31

"It's alright," he said. I looked at Mom again. She was still pretending to look out the window, like she had X-ray vision and could see through the blinds. I whimpered a bit more and Mom blinked and ran a hand through her hair. Then the pain jumped several levels as my skin tore apart. The world became fuzzy.

***

I woke up on the floor next to the examination table. Staring up at the gray, dropped ceiling, I was too dizzy to move. My body was cold everywhere. For a moment, I didn't know what had happened. I blinked a few times. Then two figures entered my view, one with a mustache and white hands, and the other a woman with her mouth open in disbelief. The mustache reached his white hands down to my body. I felt fingers on my genitals.

"He'll be alright," the doctor said, "I got all of it."

"Come on, sweetie," Mom said as she helped me to my feet. My legs shook as I stood up and Mom knelt next to me to lift my pants up.

The doctor stepped away, towards the sink. He removed the latex gloves. As he tossed them into the trash, I noticed small deposits of blood on some of the fingers. Then there was the sound of water, as he turned on the faucet, and the *clunk clunk clunk* of the soap dispenser as he tapped it with his hand. He washed himself with that awful pink soap. The type of soap that you only find at healthcare facilities and schools. The type that made my knuckles chap up in the winter.

"Zach, you're going to need to pull the skin back while it's healing. It doesn't have to always be pulled back but whenever you go pee, make sure to pull the skin all the way back for a while so that it heals without reattaching," the doctor said while facing the sink. I didn't tune anything out this time. I was willing to do whatever it took to keep him away from my dick.

We walked back to the waiting room and I told Mom I needed to pee.

"Okay, but leave the door unlocked," she said.

I went in and closed the door then caught a look of myself in the mirror. My face was pale, which made the circles under my eyes look almost like someone had punched me. I anxiously pulled my pants down to inspect the damage. It hurt so bad, but I was surprised to see most of it was unchanged, just a small amount of blood and discoloration. I pulled the skin back, which stung. The pain distracted me, and I pissed all over the toilet seat. It hadn't occurred to me to lift it.

I walked out after washing my hands and we got in the clean, white minivan and drove home. I thought, *Uncle Bobby is out of my life, but now I have to worry about the doctor.* I started pretending to be healthy when I was sick, so I wouldn't have to see him again. I also became combative during shots, hitting nurses and needing to be pinned down. I don't think I was afraid of needles. I think I just didn't trust whatever they were trying to do to me.

7

Bowser and Bootsie

Location: Maple Valley, WA
Age: 7

When the Tyrant moved in everything in the house changed. There were new hooks by the front door with a mirror that had typed on it "Patrons of this establishment are required to HANG GUNS HERE." Country music played at a low volume almost constantly. The garage was no longer vacant, occupied to the brim by Makita Power Tools, tool chests, the frame of an old truck—with some of its parts—and a bright pink electronic sign, hanging from the ceiling and always on, which read "Pretty Cool, Huh?" It smelled like cigarette smoke out there, as the Tyrant, like Papa, was a pack-and-a-half a day sort of man and the garage was the only part of the house he was permitted to smoke in.

The downstairs, formerly my place of solitude, where I would play Nintendo in relative peace, now had its walls lined with shelves of Garfield stuffed animals and other related toys. The kitchen had a small, black coffee maker in it, which gurgled loud enough that it woke me up in the morning, well before I needed to be getting ready for school or Mom's morning shift. The television had the news on, invariably broadcast by a serious-sounding man, talking about how bad things were getting. An old rifle, a whip, and a saddle hung above the TV in the living room. And an entire cabinet in the kitchen was committed to red party cups, Gilbey's gin, tonic water, and various glassware, especially a variation of a lowball glass with bulged sides.

Mom had originally been a margarita drinker, Jose Cuervo her usual brand, but she seemed to adopt gin and tonics by osmosis. Garfield became our house mascot and we all got shirts with him on it. The Tyrant's was a sleep-deprived looking Garfield on a black sweatshirt, holding an empty cup of coffee, with the text "Give me coffee and no one gets hurt." It was almost funny at first.

A white flagpole was erected in the front yard and the American flag was always raised, with two small lights shining up at it during the night. And there was an old, brown cabinet in the master bedroom with a polaroid photo of a young man holding an M-16 and a commendation medal in a box next to it.

I chafed at many of these changes but didn't dare mention it. I wasn't alone though. Our pet tabby cat, Bootsie, with the white bib and boots, took exception to other cats in the house and began targeting Garfield. She would jump atop a cabinet and up to the shelves to assault this orange intruder. Fluffy toys, the Tyrant's many treasures, would be ignominiously dumped over and down to the floor, where I would collect them and return them to their original place, admonishing Bootsie as I went.

"You don't know how mad he'll get, dumb cat," I'd say as I stood on a chair and pulled Bootsie from the ledge, before returning to the couch and my precious Mario or Zelda.

I was sitting on the couch playing *Mario Bros 3*, the tank level in the last world with ominous music, and I heard Bootsie doing her usual, hopping up to the top of the cabinet, readying another attack. I sighed and paused the game, turning my head to observe as the tabby wiggled her butt.

"HEY!" I shouted at her. She was startled, but had already committed to leap, and bounced off one of the Garfields, which wobbled, then joined her on the floor. Bootsie sat on her haunches and peered at me as if I were a traitor.

"Dumb cat," I said, as I got off the couch to retrieve the Tyrant's toy. The garage door opened.

"WHAT ARE YOU DOING!?" came a shout from behind me. It was my turn to be startled. I lowered my head into my shoulders, then turned slowly, Garfield in hand, to see who had shouted at me. An overweight bald man with a thick brown mustache stood before me.

"THOSE AREN'T FOR YOU TO PLAY WITH!" the Tyrant yelled as he advanced.

"I… I wasn't. It was Bootsie. I swear!" I pleaded as I cowered before him.

"The cat was playing with my Garfields?" The Tyrant narrowed his eyes. Then, as if on cue, the dumb cat re-launched herself atop the cabinet and wiggled her butt again.

"CAT! HEY CAT!" The Tyrant yelled, but Bootsie didn't care this time. She jumped up on the shelf and began slinking and swatting her way through the Garfields. Her goal appeared to be a porcelain Garfield near the end, which would certainly break if knocked down. The Tyrant charged past me.

Bootsie noticed as he got closer and glanced his way. The Tyrant jumped and grabbed at her with his right hand, exposing his flabby belly as he leapt. He took hold of what he could, in this case it was one of Bootsie's hind legs. The weight of his descent pulled Bootsie off the shelf, and she made a "RAOW" noise as she fell. A fluffy Garfield tumbled with her, as she clawed around in a vain attempt to secure herself.

Once on the floor, Bootsie retreated towards the TV and my precious Mario. The Tyrant charged again and Bootsie, new to conflict with people, didn't flee. He kicked her, and she bounced off the TV, making a different noise.

"REEOOWWW" Bootsie cried out in pain as she ricocheted off the screen and back to the carpet. She attempted to flee now, but the Tyrant stepped to intercept and booted her again, in the ass, causing her to cartwheel through the air towards the stairs. Bootsie cried again. This time it sounded like pleading.

Bootsie ascended the stairs, limping as fast as she could. The Tyrant continued his pursuit.

"Please stop!" I cried. The Tyrant halted, his back to me, and twisted his head to the right, then left. Then he turned around to look at me. Tension rippled through my body as I realized he might come for me now.

"WHAT?" he demanded.

"Please don't kill Bootsie."

"I'm not killing the damn cat."

"I... I'll watch her more closely from now on."

"Make sure you do," the Tyrant instructed, raising his eyebrows and staring through me.

"I will," I said. The Tyrant tilted his head back and made a forced frown, then walked back to the garage.

**

I didn't see Bootsie for several hours, until Sarah walked down the stairs. I was cheating with the white egg timer, resetting it every so often so it wouldn't ring. It was well past the half hour I was allowed to play. Mom was sunbathing outside with the sliding door closed.

"Zach?" came Sarah's little voice behind me.

"Yes, Sarah?" I sighed, annoyed to be interrupted from fighting Bowser. It was the first time I'd faced him in this version of Mario. And I'd died a lot to get here.

"Bootsie won't come out."

"What?" I paused the game and turned around. Sarah was carrying one of her Barbie dolls and a small comb.

"She's hiding under my bed and when I try to get her, she hisses." I turned back to the TV and cried a little.

"What's wrong?" Sarah asked.

"It's nothing," I said. I wiped at my eyes as I walked towards her.

"Let's see about Bootsie," I said as Sarah followed me upstairs.

Bootsie was never the same. She became one of those skittish cats that avoids being touched. Even when she wanted pets, she would wince on the first few brushes, until her mind let her forget what had happened. The Tyrant eventually made all of us like that.

8

The Spider

Location: Kent, WA
Age: 7

Back at Papa's apartment, things were going from bad to worse. He was having digestion issues, which he believed to be related to a bout of bladder cancer he had earlier in life.

"They might have to roto rooter me again," Papa said standing in the doorway. It sounded serious, so I looked down at the dirty, turquoise carpet. Sarah stood behind him, waiting just outside. She was sipping a cherry Slurpee from the 7-11 down the street from the apartment.

"Don't worry," he said.

"What does it mean?" I asked, looking up.

"Well, basically it means they put a tube up my penis and it has little blades on the end that rotate really fast and it cuts the tumor inside me. And then I piss constantly for a few weeks but don't die." It sounded normal to him.

"Oh," I said with a nervous laugh.

"You sure you don't wanna come?" Papa asked. I didn't ever want to go back to the doctor's office.

"No. Can I wait here please?"

"Sure. I called Bobby to come by and check on you while I'm gone." I froze. *Oh God.* Papa turned and walked away before I could respond. And little Sarah, three years my junior but apparently wiser, left with him, Slurpee straw still in her mouth.

I heard the van door close and knew I had made a huge mistake. *The doctor won't do anything to me unless I have an appointment. I should have gone. I could have just waited in the lobby.* It was too late, and I felt so stupid. Papa drove away.

I sat down on the brown couch with the pink and blue stains from Gak and Silly Putty. Considering my options, I didn't see a way out. The only thing I could think of was to call Mom and tell her Uncle Bobby was coming by. She had warned Papa about that. *Maybe she'd come rescue me.* I leapt off the couch.

I picked up the phone from the nightstand next to Papa's bed. It smelled terrible in his room, like diarrhea and cigarettes. I squinted in the direction of the bathroom adjoining his bedroom. *Did he not flush?* Lifting my shirt up to cover my mouth and nose, I quickly dialed my home phone number and waited. It rang and rang and rang. Answering machine. Mom wasn't home. I tried again. Same result. Again? Answering machine a third time. I tried some more, sitting on the edge of Papa's bed with shaking legs, but eventually gave up.

Accepting my fate, I walked back to the brown couch and turned on the television. Nickelodeon. Something to take my mind off the feeling of impending doom that was encompassing me. Before long, the front door opened, and in walked my destroyer. He was here to care for me.

Uncle Bobby stood there in the doorway, right where Papa had been moments before, and narrowed his eyes at me. A monster with a combover and mustache and a better wardrobe than my slovenly father. I was terrified. It must have shown.

"Zachary… it's been… a long while," he began, with a wide smile and the tone of a prison guard who abuses inmates.

"Hello," I replied, like an inmate who hopes today isn't one of those days.

"So, your Papa is sick, eh?" he closed and locked the door. I could hear the faint sound of the lock sliding into place.

"Yes, he says they might rotor him again."

"What?"

"Something bad about his stomach."

"Oh," he approached me without taking off his shoes. I always noticed that he and Papa didn't take off their shoes inside like you're supposed to. *That doesn't matter though. The carpet is already gross.*

"What are you watching?"

"Nickelodeon. *Doug.*"

"Hmmm. Want to play a game?" He patted me on the shoulder, smiling even more.

Oh no. He's going to take his time with it. At this point, I had concluded that if this was my fate, I'd prefer immediate pain, like what happened at the Chinese restaurant, as opposed to the phoniness of contact ostensibly done for mutual entertainment, like the pool or reading with me on his lap or whatever this was about to be. I didn't yet have the capacity to formulate it succinctly in my mind like that, but the feeling was the same. *The whole point of his games is to get close to me, so he can do bad things. If no one is here, and no one can save me, why doesn't he just get on with it?* I thought of Snow White and the tricks that were played by the evil queen to try and kill her. It never made sense to me as a child that someone who seems all-powerful would resort to deception as if they were still afraid of being caught. *Why bother with tricks if no one can stop you?*

"Hmmm?" He asked.

"Okay. How about... hide and seek?" I suggested the only game where I could possibly escape.

"Well, alright."

"I'm It. I'll count to thirty."

"Oh... okay," he sounded displeased but got up and went to hide while I counted.

"One... Two... Three..." I counted slowly but not so much as to cause suspicion. I lowered my head during but cheated and looked past my arm hairs to see Uncle Bobby walk into Papa's room, then out of it and into the playroom. *He thinks Papa's room stinks too.*

Time passed as I counted, as slow as I could. Towards the end, I dragged my heels more, by adding halves and three quarters to the count.

"Twenty-eight... twenty-eight and a half... twenty-eight and three quarters... twenty-nine... twenty-nine and a half... twenty-nine and three quarters... ... ... thirty."

I looked up and glanced around, then after a few moments slid off the couch and sauntered to Papa's room. Sitting on his bed again in that dark, dusty room, shirt pulled up over the nose, I waited as long as I could without arousing suspicion or vomiting, then walked out of it to the kitchen. I played dumb, loudly opening small cupboards as if this child thought an adult could hide in there. Then the refrigerator, which I immediately regretted doing. There was nothing in it but spoiled sausage links and an expired carton of orange juice. It smelled like mold and cold. I closed it and wiped my nose in disgust.

I walked towards the front door and noticed a small beam of light under the playroom door to my left. It hadn't been lit up before. *He's getting impatient.*

Instead, I went to the bathroom and flung the shower curtain to the side. I tried to not look at the floor tiles, for fear of remembering, as I opened the small cupboards underneath the sink. A whistling began in the playroom. With nowhere else to search, I exited the bathroom and turned the knob to the playroom door. The whistling stopped. I turned the knob back and forth, as if the door was locked or something was blocking it. It was the second-to-last attempt I made at delaying the inevitable.

During one of the turns, the door pulled away from me and opened a hair. I sighed and walked in. It was worse than I expected. Uncle Bobby stood there in the middle of the room with his penis hanging out from his pants. He smiled.

"You found me!" he exclaimed in a childlike voice. I gasped and took a step back and stared at it for a moment. It started to bob up and down, as if my shock was doing something to it.

"Come here," Uncle Bobby said. I took a small, reluctant step towards him, then thought better of it.

"You're it!" I said to him, then turned and ran away to hide.

"Hey, wait a second!" Uncle Bobby protested.

"Start counting!" I shouted from down the hall. I was heading to Papa's room, hoping to use the stench as a deterrent.

I reached Papa's bedroom door and heard Uncle Bobby counting quickly in frustration. "One. Two. Three. Four." A plan formed in my mind. I closed Papa's door without entering his room, then backtracked with light feet and hid in the living room. Laying down in front of the smaller of two brown couches, I was out of view from someone approaching from the kitchen or playroom but was otherwise hiding in plain sight.

Uncle Bobby counted to thirty quickly and then exited the playroom. He noticed Papa's door was closed and walked to it. Peering from the floor, just barely poking my head out from the couch, I could see a smirk on his face.

The sound of the door opening was the sign to make my move. I pulled one of the couch cushions off and stacked it on the couch haphazardly, then moved with light feet towards the playroom,

43

pausing briefly to peer down the hall to see if he was searching Papa's room. The door to Papa's bathroom opened and I heard Uncle Bobby say "Wow" in disgust. I made it all the way to the playroom and hid behind the old mattresses that functioned as my wrestling ring.

There was a spider down there, against the wall with me, about a foot from my face. It crawled around in its dusty little web, which was devoid of fresh food, much like Papa's fridge. I imagined the spider was looking at me. Was he complaining about the lack of nourishment?

"How can a place this dirty not have any flies for me to eat?" the spider might ask.

"A good point, Mr. Spider," I might reply. Or was he looking at me as if I were a fly?

"Don't. Please don't," I whispered to Papa's roommate. *I am already food for another.*

The playroom door opened, and I winced, hoping Uncle Bobby hadn't heard my voice. The light switch flicked, and the room went dark. There was the sound of footsteps, but they didn't sound like they were getting closer, more like moving from one side of the room to the other. The playroom closet door opened and there was rummaging amongst Papa's old jackets. The second playroom door, leading to the bathroom, opened and I heard cupboards, then footsteps in the kitchen and more cupboards opening and closing. A child could actually fit in some of those places.

I looked for the spider again. In the dark, I imagined he was crawling closer to me. *I am not your food, Mr. Spider.* I heard footsteps again but couldn't tell where they were. I was focused on finding the spider and couldn't shake the thought that there were others, that maybe they were already crawling on me.

Peering over the old mattresses, I surveyed the room as best I could in the dark. I didn't know where Uncle Bobby was, but he didn't seem to be here. I got up quickly and said goodbye to Mr.

Spider, then walked around the old mattresses, along the faded red-and-gold Persian rug, to the playroom closet that had already been searched.

Stepping inside, amongst the old jackets, I brushed my arms and neck to remove the phantom spiders. Content there were none, I let out a sigh of relief. I felt that maybe I had fooled him, or at least delayed things enough that Papa would return in time. I didn't feel safe, but I felt safer than before.

"GOTCHA!" the old jackets yelled as they wrapped their arms around me. I shrieked in horror.

"It's okay. It's okay." Uncle Bobby reassured me as he held me in his arms. This spider reached with one hand to the closet door and slowly closed it with both of us inside. I hadn't been clever enough.

"I found you," Uncle Bobby said in the childlike voice again. I said nothing in return.

"Here. Remember how I showed you?" He took my hand and placed it on his penis and moved my hand with his. I complied. He reached with his other hand into my pants and fondled my genitals with his fingers.

"… no," I murmured.

"It's okay," he insisted, as he lowered my pants. He stepped behind me, pulling his penis away from my hand, squatted, and began rubbing it up and down on my backside. *What's he doing?* I feared where this was going. I thought of the Polaroid photos of my ass.

For the first time, I did something on my own during the abuse. I reached behind and took hold of his penis and started stroking it again.

"Oh," Uncle Bobby said, "Good boy."

I turned my body to the side so that I could move more freely, and to position my ass away from him. He stood up again. I started stroking as fast as I could.

"Oh, that's a very good boy," Uncle Bobby said, his breathing becoming heavy. My ass was safe, though he still had one hand on it, clutching a cheek.

He eventually came on one of Papa's old jackets and I was able to slip away from him while he was still feeling overwhelmed. I went back to the living room and resumed watching Nickelodeon. Another episode of *Doug* was on.

A few minutes later, Uncle Bobby emerged from the playroom, perspiration streaking down his face.

"Do you need anything?" He asked me, wiping his forehead.

"No," I replied. He turned and left. I tried to watch *Doug* through my tears. They started flowing right after the door closed.

I never saw him again. Papa said he won the lottery and moved somewhere warm. I guess that's like the "Your dog lives on a farm now" story, only for pedophiles that are still alive.

9

Special Place

Location: Maple Valley, WA
Age: 8

I attended Rock Creek Elementary School for first through sixth grade. My first few years there, I had a counselor that I saw once a week to help me deal with the divorce. I was having a lot of anger issues back then and used to wake up in the middle of the night attacking Mom's bedroom door with my toy ninja sword. I don't remember getting out of bed but would just be at the door already attacking. I would scream all sorts of things until she unlocked the door and grabbed my sword and hit me with it until I ran back to my room crying. In school, I didn't make very many friends, as I generally fluctuated between crying and yelling, neither of which elicit much contact from others. After Mom married the Tyrant, I stopped attacking her door because he could hit a lot harder and seemed to enjoy it while Mom had always been sad about it.

He convinced her to close the small business she was running. Mom was self-sufficient before then, but he preyed on her insecurities and pressured her to let him be the provider. "A single woman can't make it on her own with two kids," was part of his marriage sales pitch, then later "I make enough money that you should stay home more. The kids need it." So, she closed her business then got a part-time job as a lunch lady at the school after the Tyrant came up short on bills. Money was tight, and Mom gave me free meals in the cafeteria.

Mom picked up some early morning shifts at the school by serving breakfast. It was a program for low-income kids that allowed them to get free or reduced-price food. Mom woke me up every morning at six to go with her. That way I could eat too. I don't want to make it sound like we were living hand to mouth or something. We weren't. We lived in a decent suburb; Mom and the Tyrant both had jobs, although he was unemployed a few times and brought a lot of credit card debt with him.

I made a few friends from Cub Scouts—joining the scouts was the only good thing the Tyrant made me do—but none of them were in the breakfast program. So, I would grab my French Toast sticks or cereal or whatever and go off in a corner and eat alone by a cart of encyclopedias. Out of sheer boredom, I picked up one of these books at random and started thumbing through it. I grabbed the M book and eventually found my way to the Middle Ages. I was fascinated by all the weapons and castles and the stories of all the different wars fought for this crown or that religion, though there were some parts I didn't understand. I started to incorporate what I read into my Lego castle designs at home, but I never had enough blocks to build the Krak des Chevaliers.

After exhausting the encyclopedias—including a detour to read just enough about spiders to become arachnophobic—I rented all the castle books I could find in the school library or the Maple Valley library. I read about the Crusades and different civil wars and how castle designs had evolved from Roman times. My favorite book was a shorter one with drawings showing all the different rooms and jobs in a typical castle. I always felt bad for that one lonely guy who had to shovel all the poop that fell down the long, stone shaft.

At school, I used free play time and recess to read more about castles and to make rudimentary drawings of my own designs. This kept me isolated, which my teacher thought might be bad for me. "You need to go play with the other kids at recess," she said, and I was sent out.

I hated going outside back then. During one of the many times Mom took me to the doctor's office, it was discovered that I had asthma and allergies. I was given an albuterol inhaler, with a blue collapsible spacer, and scheduled for allergy shots. The shots turned out to be a rather imprecise practice, where I ended up feeling more like a participant in medical experiments than a patient receiving medical treatment. One of the 38 allergies I had was grass, and the grass field at school always seemed freshly cut. Recess usually resulted in me having a runny nose and itchy eyes for an hour after.

Some of the boys at school had a game they played called "French Greetings." It was more like a ritual they did to each other. We had learned at an assembly what a French kiss was; it was just a strong kiss with tongue. Some sixth graders in the row in front of us told us. We also learned what a greeting was while learning how to write cursive in class. "It's like the written version of a handshake," the teacher said.

This small group of boys, about six of them, had created something called "French Greetings" which was a more intimate form of saying hello, to them anyways. Whenever they saw one of their crew, they would walk up and grab him by the crotch while giggling "French Greetings." It scared the hell out of me, so I avoided them constantly.

When I was forced out of the classroom and away from my drawings and books, I walked slowly up the bus lane to the playground and field, scanning for this strange crew of kids from my class. I saw them playing kickball, so I went to the swings. Other days, I saw them playing with the tire swing, so I played kickball. This was my usual routine for quite a while, always on the lookout for them and trying to keep as much distance as I could. I would see them grabbing each other by the crotch and laughing. Every now and then one would grab too hard, causing the other to fall to the ground in pain. *Animals*.

I started hiding castle books in my shirt and taking them to recess with me. I would sit under the slide next to a large tic-tac-toe and read by myself. I chose that location because I noticed that the crew was never by it. It was isolated and dirty, but sunlight still filtered in through the little holes in the playground floor above. It smelled like rubber and woodchips down there, and other kids running above would cause dust and dirt to drift down, but I was safe.

I got complacent and one day I looked up and saw the six boys playing on the monkey bars right next to me. I stared for a moment, then slowly got up and tried to slink away. Their leader, Tommy, saw what I was doing, smirked, and said something to the others. They started to approach, I ran, and they gave chase.

They tried to corner me on the playground. I pushed a tire swing towards them and ran across the field, through a game of flyer's up and then in between the portables. The school was overcrowded, and we had six portables. I got away, or so I thought, and hid behind the large green dumpster next to the school. It smelled like rotten fish and vomit back there. I was wheezing and pulled out my inhaler to take a puff. I hid there for a few minutes, but I soon heard them walking around on the other side of it. There were only two ways out, as it was pressed up against the concrete wall of the school. They were tactical. They came from both sides.

With his comrades blocking my only exits, Tommy approached me.

"Don't you want to be friends?" He asked.

"Sure…"

"Then why won't you play with us? Why always read?"

"It's my special place and you're not supposed to touch it," I said, reciting what we had learned in one of those "bad touch" videos at school.

He didn't listen. Knowing I wasn't going to cooperate, he called two more boys to behind the dumpster. "New member," Tommy said and pointed at me. They grabbed my arms and held them. Tommy then walked up and instead of grabbing the outside, he unzipped me and slid his hand inside my pants. "French Greetings" he whispered.

I was scared. I thought he was going to hurt me like the doctor. I struggled to get away but the two holding me were too strong. "No," I pleaded in a whisper as I struggled to free myself. I didn't dare to shout. I thought everyone would make fun of me. He held my penis and rubbed it back and forth like Uncle Bobby.

"Greetings" he whispered again.

The rubbing caused a sensation I had never experienced before. My body was tingling and my crotch was inflating somehow. It felt wrong and I was confused by it. I became dizzy. My legs were like jelly. I tried to say "No" again but no words came. He rubbed faster and faster, while I remained frozen in place. Then, the recess whistle blew. Tommy let go and ran away with the others, back to class. I collapsed to the ground with my pants sliding partly down. As I lay there, some of the dirty water from the dumpster soaked my pant leg.

I laid there sobbing for a while. Eventually a recess teacher, one of those old ladies in an orange reflective vest, came along and saw me. "What's wrong with you?" she asked. My face flushed with shame. I got up and ran to the boy's bathroom to inspect myself, then down to my counselor's office in tears, but I wouldn't tell her anything and was sent back to class.

When I sat down in class, I saw the book I took to recess was inside my desk. I hadn't realized I dropped it. One of the nice girls had seen what happened and brought it back for me. Her name was Rebecca and she had long black hair. She leaned over, "Are you okay?" I started to cry again and was sent to the nurse's office to deal with my pants.

As I left, Tommy and one of the other boys turned back, smiled, and mouthed "Greetings."

I didn't tell anyone about what happened at recess. My father was still distant. My stepfather had hit me a week or so prior for refusing to empty the trash. My mother realized she had made a mistake in marrying him but was terrified of what he might do if she tried to end it. Also, as time went by, I detected more and more my mother's guilt about divorcing my father. It first showed in her eyes, then her face, and finally her voice. She considered the divorce a failure, which made her hesitant to consider doing it again.

The teachers at school cared, but they also got overwhelmed by all my emotions and the things I wouldn't tell them. "If you won't tell me anything, I can't help you," was their usual refrain. I hated them for that, that they wanted to force me to do things their way when I was the one in pain. I needed to submit to their adult system, a system that had already failed me multiple times, a system I had zero trust in, in order to achieve safety. I accepted again that I was on my own and this was the way of the world.

***

At recess the next day, I went about my normal routine and sat under the slide with the castle book from my desk. A few of the nice girls from class and a tired looking boy who played with them came by and sat with me. I didn't know what to say and they didn't either. We sat in silence, the girls drawing in little notebooks and the tired boy taking a nap, using his red hoody as a pillow. This went on for a few days but eventually they were drawn away to play basketball and I was alone again. Then, that crew of six returned.

I tried to get my teacher to let me stay inside, but quickly learned this was another time where I was required to be somewhere that was unsafe. *People only force you to be somewhere if it's bad for you,* I thought, furthering my incipient worldview about authority and demands.

***

I experienced "French Greetings" numerous more times but none as bad as the first. I didn't run from it, as I knew they had me beat at that. There was clearly nowhere for a husky asthmatic like me to hide out there either. I contemplated going to the field and staying close to one of the recess ladies but figured that would only anger the crew and they'd get to me eventually anyways. I gave up. A few weeks of mistreatment went by and then I was saved by Christmas Break.

10

All I want for Christmas is to Die

Location: Maple Valley & Kent, WA
Age: 8-9

Christmas in my home was like Hell papered over with nice decorations, plenty of food, and country music blaring throughout the house. I had a break from my tormentors at recess but the place I went to take that break had a different type of tormentor in it, my stepfather. So many of my problems in childhood occurred in the places I was required by authority to be.

We got a little snow that Christmas, which is rare in the Pacific Northwest. I wanted to make a castle out of it and went to the backyard to build, so no one from the neighborhood could knock it over. I grabbed a small disc sled to shuttle snow from the front yard to the back and began piling it up to make walls. Then, I moved a large, blue tote from the garage, flipped it over, and piled snow on top of it, then made walls there too. My Lego knights got added to the tote section, as this was the keep. I put archers on the lower wall, so they could defend. I was feeling pretty content with my creation and sat down to look at it for a minute.

A snowball came flying over me from behind and smashed through part of the walls, then hit the keep, hurling my knights in all directions. I turned around and saw the Tyrant, chuckling to himself, a red cup in hand, full of his usual gin and tonic I assumed, in sweatpants and that black Garfield sweatshirt. He made a dumb smile.

"This is a siege," he hollered at me.

"I don't want to play." I went back to the tote and began rebuilding the wall and retrieving my downed knights. Another snowball flew in and this time it was the archers who were struck. I got angry. He threw a snowball with a bit of ice the first time. That was how it penetrated my defenses. The second was a softer, grazing blow along the top of the outer wall. I cupped the ice together while pretending to retrieve the Lego men behind the tote. He turned around to find more snow. I hurled my ice ball at him just as he turned back to me, cup raised for a sip. It was a direct hit. The cup splashed his face and then dropped to the ground. Part of the ice had hit him in the face too. I knew I was in trouble and ran inside through the sliding back door, tracking snow through the house, and up the stairs to the bathroom, locking the door behind. I always hid in one of the bathrooms, as the bedrooms didn't have locks. My inhaler was also in there. I grabbed it from the drawer and took a puff.

The problem is that the doorknob on the other side had a little hole in it that you could shove a toothpick through to unlock it. I didn't know that. A safety feature I suppose, though it only made me feel unsafe. The Tyrant trudged up the stairs, checked my bedroom, then realizing I wasn't there, turned his attention to the bathroom. He started knocking and yelling when he found out I locked the door.

"Open up NOW," he demanded, with fists hitting the door.

"I just wanted to play alone," I pleaded.

He had a Swiss army knife. It had a toothpick that you could pull out. He pulled it out and I heard the doorknob make a *POP* noise and unlock. Shocked, I tried to get to the door to lock it again. He turned the knob and threw the door open. It hit me in the face. I stumbled backwards, fell, and hit my shoulder on the bathtub. I cried out.

"DON'T EVER DO THAT AGAIN!" he screamed. He moved in, leaned down, and slapped me. I yelped and started to cry more.

"STOP CRYING LIKE A LITTLE GIRL!" his face was red and that brown mustache wet with gin and ice and anger. He slapped me again and I curled up in a ball next to the toilet, peeking out at him behind my arms. He just stood there after that, judging me, shaming me for not being more of a man. I turned nine a few days later.

Mom was little help back then. There was a real before-and-after shot of her relationship, with him being sweet and considerate before the wedding, then dropping credit card debt and abuse after. She had proceeded from the shock phase of that and was now working on appeasement, allowing him the parental authority he so craved and with it the right to hand out his own style of discipline. She required my sister and I to say "I love you" to him and give him a hug every evening before bed. Sarah had to kiss him, too, since she was a girl.

Mom acquiesced to him taking us to another room when we were bad, the noises coming from it telling her without doubt what was happening to us. Appeasement never works. I often heard them arguing downstairs, even during the holidays. His voice would be the raised one and hers the little, imploring one.

***

The days between the snowball incident and my birthday, I avoided family as best I could. I spent evenings in my room, pretending to play, and during the day I would walk to the other side of my neighborhood and sit alone on a curb and cry. *I'm trapped.* School was a nightmare and so was home. I had no control of either. I had no control over my life at all. *Why are people so bad to me? What did I ever do?* I thought about the future, the next few years of school, and how my family would be. Everything I could come up with showed me a lack of recourse. Unlike with homework, video games, and my toy castles, there seemed to be problems in my life that I could not solve. Problems that made life not worth living. *Maybe no one loves me after all.*

***

Birthdays and holidays were always split between Mom's house and Papa's apartment. After Uncle Bobby stopped coming by, Papa had let the place go even worse than before. I don't think it had been vacuumed in months. It had likely never been dusted. The turquoise carpet was discolored and had old leaves and sandwich wrappers and who knows what else from fall and summer. Dust and mold were two of my allergies. Mom had given up scolding Papa about cleanliness and smoking around kids. The Tyrant's berating had taken all the fight out of her. She was cowed, even around the old, depressed, slob that was my father. Instead, she had me take my albuterol inhaler, with the blue collapsible spacer, so I could take larger puffs if the decrepit dwelling took its toll on my breathing.

On December 30th, Papa took us out for dinner at *Azteca*, where I got the usual birthday song with the sombrero and all that. After dinner, we sat there and waited as he finished the last of his martinis. Then, he swerved us back to his place, so I could open the presents that Mom had bought for me with his money, because

57

he was too lazy to go shopping but could always hand out cash. Along the way, he lit up a smoke and a whiff of it got taken in by Sarah, who coughed. It gave me an idea. I thought of my inhaler and a way out.

I opened my presents at the apartment. A small Lego castle, a Seahawks shirt, and some candy. Not a bad haul. I told myself not to look, not to ruin the moment and confirm again how little he cared for me. But, I couldn't help it. I snatched the little To/From labels off the wrapping and inspected them. I learned things about my father the same way I learned Santa wasn't real. There's no way my mother's handwriting could be the same as my father's. There's no way Santa could have different handwriting at my friend's house. And how could my father, a man that couldn't be bothered to vacuum his apartment or empty the trash, wrap these presents up perfectly, and with the same exact wrapping paper Mom used? *How stupid do they think I am?*

"Thank you for the presents, Papa," I pretended to be grateful.

"You're welcome, Zechariah." He called me that sometimes, as it was what he wanted to name me. He liked it because it was biblical. He was the most nominal Catholic.

What a phony my father is. I'll show him. I'll show them all. Papa got a bottle from the fridge and went to his bedroom. I put *Monkey Trouble* on for Sarah, turned the volume up, then took my presents and inhaler with me to the playroom. I closed the door and started to cry.

"God, if you're here, please just kill me," I whimpered.

I waited for a moment, then said it again. When I realized no lightning bolt was in the offing, I dropped the candy and Legos to the floor, then laid down on the dingy, old red-and-gold Persian rug, resting my head on my new Seahawks shirt. I contemplated the revolver but knew there was no ammo. *Why do people lie when they don't have to? Why are the people in charge of me so bad? Is it going to be this way my whole life?*

The collapsible spacer was a large chamber that a regular inhaler cartridge attaches to. It allows multiple puffs of the inhaler to be stored in the chamber, so you can take one large, long puff at once. I remembered my sister coughing in the van from Papa's cigarette smoke and the doctor telling me not to overdo it when he first prescribed me albuterol. I laid there on the floor for a moment and thought about my life and how I felt about leaving it. I looked at the off-white walls and the two doors. One led to my distracted sister and phony father. The other led to the bathroom where Uncle Bobby started in with me a few years before. I thought of the kids at school and their French Greetings, and the doctor, and how much I hated the Tyrant but could not escape him. I realized that I hated my mother also, that even if she was hurt too, it had been her decisions that put us on this path. I rejected her the moment she divorced Papa and cried on her wedding day, begging her not to marry the Tyrant.

I concluded that I had nowhere to run to and no one to turn to and that my only solution was in my hand.

Standing up, I held the spacer and plugged in the cartridge. I didn't know how many puffs it would take, so I pressed over and over and over until the flexible chamber walls became firm. Then, I wiped my tears, breathed out as hard as I could, held the end to my mouth, and inhaled.

Some of the effects were instantaneous. I couldn't breathe, couldn't even finish the full pull from the chamber. My chest pounded. My hand shook and felt heavy and I dropped the spacer. I fell to the ground without realizing it. A small wisp of vapor coming from the end of the spacer was the last thing I clearly saw. Then there was a tingly feeling all over my body and my head hurt and I saw flickering lights along the rug my face was on. *Oh God, what have I done?* My brain sent commands to my legs to kick the wall for help, but I don't know if they followed their orders or not.

I couldn't feel them anymore. *Is this it?* I slipped away into unconsciousness.

***

Sometime later, the door opened, and the light flickered off and on, off and on. A fat, bald man in sweatpants stood in the doorway.

"Taking a nap, Zechariah?" He asked.

I felt groggy and weak. My head was fuzzy and my chest felt like it had been punched. There was cold sweat on my forehead. *Did I die? Is this God?* I focused my vision and realized it was just my father.

"Come on son, it's time for me to take you back to your mother's."

I struggled to my feet, collected my presents, and slowly walked to the door. I didn't tell anyone what I had done. During the drive home, I pushed out the back window a crack and, when a semi-truck with bright lights blinded the old man for a moment, I dropped the spacer to the street below.

***

"STOP DOING PRESENTS FOR PAPA!" I yelled at Mom as I walked in the front door. She looked for a moment, shocked.

"How was your birthday at Papa's?" she asked.

"IT WAS A LIE!" I yelled.

"Okay, calm down, Zach," Mom said. Sarah squinted up at me.

"It's just like Santa. It's the same handwriting as yours and the same wrapping paper. Santa is a lie and so is Papa!"

"Santa's a lie?" Sarah asked.

"No, he isn't," Mom looked down at her. I dropped my presents and kicked off my shoes towards the shoe rack.

"YES HE IS AND SO IS PAPA!" I yelled.

"What's going on?" The Tyrant walked up from the den. I frowned at him.

"Zach's upset about his birthday at Frosty's," Mom informed him.

"Not like what you got?" he asked.

"I DON'T LIKE THAT IT'S A LIE!"

"HEY! What did we talk about?" he asked. I started to cry and ran for the stairs. He grabbed at my arm. I shook loose and kept running.

"I hate you," I said as I went up the stairs. I didn't specify who it was towards.

The Tyrant followed me upstairs. I tried to hold my door shut but he was too strong. The door burst open and he was on me. I was lifted into the air and spun around. Then my body came to a stop, hovering above the ground, my eyes trained on the floor and a pressure on my belly, bent over his knee. My pants were pulled down, then I heard the *swoosh* with a sting after each one. He spanked me until I yelped. It was the only sound that made him stop.

"Now come here," he said afterwards, kneeling, with his arms open.

"What?"

"Come here."

I obeyed, and he hugged me, and I didn't like it.

***

By the time January rolled around, I was desperate to get back to school. A few days after the snowball incident, the day after my birthday, New Year's Eve, the Tyrant took me to the garage and hit me and showed me his gun collection. Even a child can pick up that message, though he didn't realize I'd already tried to beat him to it.

I got back to school and went to recess expecting the worst, and there was no abuse whatsoever. It turns out one of the boys from that crew had done a "French Greeting" to a cousin or something over the holidays. He got caught and fessed up to his parents and they told some of the parents from the other boys and now none of them were doing it. I started to love school again but still felt unsafe at home.

11

Elvira

Location: Kent, WA
Age: 9

In spring and summertime, the family would pile into our white Ford Taurus hatchback in the wee hours of the morning and make our way to the Midway Swap Meet. It was about a half hour away in Kent. We went at least once every weekend.

Sarah and I didn't like waking up early, especially when it wasn't a school day, but we knew protesting would do us no good. We slept in the car on the way there or munched on Cheerios and poppy seed muffins that Mom packed in Ziplock bags for our breakfast. K106.1, which was a country station back then, would play at a low volume the whole way there and back. Probably Garth Brooks or Reba.

The swap meet was one of the things the Tyrant loved to do. He loved to haggle with the vendors—he *had to* do it—even for stuff we didn't need. Getting a good deal, even if it meant taking advantage of someone, made him feel good. And he'd brag to Mom later. "See what a good deal I got on that chair?"

"Yes, honey," Mom would reply.

We parked the Taurus and stepped out, making our way to the black pavement and line after line of vendors. Vendors of all types. Clothing, cabinets, old televisions, W.W.F. and W.C.W. wrestling cards (my favorites), tables, chairs, more clothes, you name it. They even had a few vendors with Nintendo games, some that I hadn't played or even heard of, like *Kid Icarus*. We walked along these rows of vendors, most of whom were overweight and worse-for-wear, in our matching jean jackets and the Tyrant wearing his camouflage baseball cap.

He was a pro at walking the line between interested and indifferent, walking up to vendor after vendor, glancing at their wares, lifting his chin slightly and asking "Whatcha got there?"

"Oh, used television, only a few years old. Still works just fine," came the eager reply from those who were worse off than us. They had dark circles under their sad little eyes.

Or it would be a table, "still sturdy, we just don't need it anymore," another eager vendor would say.

"Hmmmm," The Tyrant would reply, tilting his head to the side, frowning deliberately, as if weighing the person and the product at the same time. He'd let the silence do the work for him, maintaining that pensive frown, accentuated by his mustache, as we slowly walked away from the vendor.

"I'm trying to sell it for twenty-five, but I can go lower," or something similar, almost all of them would say.

If it was something he wanted, he'd pause and tilt his head to the other side, as if mulling over what a reasonable price would be. "What can you do?" he'd ask, suddenly staring through their faces.

"Oh... well... I mean I can knock it down to twenty if that works," would come the hesitant, uncomfortable reply.

"Ooooh," the Tyrant would say. He'd wince then and suck air through his teeth to make a displeased hissing noise.

"Maybe I'll come back to ya," he'd say, dismissively, nose and eyebrows scrunched, as we resumed walking. The vendors always looked so dejected when we walked away.

If it was something that he just had to have, he'd make a point to stop and talk up another vendor in the same row, within earshot of the original vendor he'd talked to. This way he could come back later, talk to this vendor, the one with the thing he didn't want, and then casually glance over, as if suddenly remembering it, and say to the original vendor, "You still got that TV?"

"Oh yeah, right here," they'd say, getting up off a small cooler they were using as a chair.

"What were we thinking on that?" The price would be lower then, as it was later in the day.

"I was... I was thinking fifteen if you can swing it," they'd say. The air sucking noise would come again.

"See my kid over here really wants some donuts and that's a few bucks," The Tyrant would point over at me, turning me into his accomplice as he robbed these poor people, "And we've already got six TVs. This is just something I was thinking for the kitchen for when my wife cooks." He'd point at Mom, who would smile uncomfortably, drafted to be an accomplice as well.

"Oh I see."

"Yeah. So, could ya do ten?"

"I... yeah I suppose so," the vendor would look down.

"Well alright then," the Tyrant would say, pulling out his wallet, which had plenty of smaller bills in it, but he'd still ask them if they could break a twenty. One last reminder of who was who in this exchange.

"Sure, let me grab some cash from the van," they'd turn around and saunter back to their little old van, usually with faded paint, and re-emerge moments later with the least crisp bills you'd ever seen. The Tyrant would raise his eyebrows and "hmph" at their bills, then carefully straighten them out and place them back in his wallet, counting its contents in front of them as he did.

"You know where that coffee place is? I need to wash my hands," he'd say, rubbing his hands on his jeans, hands that had touched their money. We'd been there a million times before. I could find that coffee place in my sleep.

"Yeah. Just walk to the end of this row," the vendor would point his arm out, "and then turn left. It's got an orange roof. Can't miss it."

"Thank you," The Tyrant would say with a large smile, as he picked up the little TV and led us away.

Mom, Sarah, and I would always be a few feet behind him when he was talking to the vendors. Better to just let him do his thing, then make your own purchases, like the time I paid face value for wrestling cards.

When the Tyrant found out I'd paid face value he was irate. He snagged my arm and dragged me up and down the rows until I confessed which vendor I'd bought from. The haggard man selling cards tried to utter "no refunds" but the Tyrant was well beyond talking. He ripped my pants down while I was still standing, then threw my cards on the pavement. They scattered and some landed face up. The only one I could clearly see was Ric Flair. These were W.C.W. cards, which wasn't even the company I was loyal to. Then there was a slap on my behind from callused hands and I stumbled forward. I caught a brief glimpse of a wide-eyed vendor, shocked by what was unfolding, fidgeting his hands. Then all I saw was black pavement, as I went over the knee like usual and the *whoosh* sound began in earnest. In between each sting I opened my eyes and saw small pieces of broken pavement scattered over the rest like sprinkles on a cake. It went on longer than any of the other times, well past the point I yelped, well past the point where my tears fell to the ground. It went on until a sudden burst of feet on pavement, and a pause in the action, and the sound of money exchanging hands. Yes, it was better to let the Tyrant do the negotiating.

We followed him down the row. He was marching now and proud, this small TV tucked under his left arm. A black man approached. I'd seen him before. He had a jean jacket on too, with some off-white fluff on the collar. His eyes darted around a lot, like he was always looking for someone. He and the Tyrant were about the same age.

"Howdy!" The Tyrant announced.

"Oh, how you doing today?" The black man replied in a deep voice.

"Just got myself a new TV. Ha ha," The Tyrant chuckled, "Gonna grab some coffee. You?"

"Actually coffee sounds good." The black man walked alongside the Tyrant as we approached the coffee building. They were chatting a little about something, but I couldn't hear it.

It wasn't just a coffee building. The Midway Swap Meet had been a drive-in movie theatre back when that was a thing, and the company that owned it had turned it into a swap meet later. The coffee building had beige walls on the outside, and a faded orange roof that hung over the sidewalk below. Inside, you could get coffee, other refreshments, donuts, and play pinball. The place smelled like warm glazed donuts. I always felt at ease when I was in there. Except this time.

We walked in and strolled over to our usual table, the one in the corner. The Tyrant plopped the "new" TV down on the table, Mom and Sarah sat down.

"You need anything, honey?" The Tyrant asked, with a beaming smile.

"No, I'm alright," Mom replied and smiled back at him. The Tyrant walked over to the line with his black friend and they got some coffee.

"I need to pee," I told Mom.

"Okay, go ahead." She tilted her head towards the men's room. I was old enough to go on my own now.

There was a line for the urinals, and the little one I usually used was taken by a heavyset, pasty man with a raggedy red hat, probably a vendor. He seemed to be struggling to pee and made a grunting noise, then looked up at the ceiling, wincing. I waited for him to finish. The door behind me opened and the Tyrant walked in. Red hat finished and walked out without washing his hands. I walked up to the urinal and started doing my business.

"You look ridiculous," The Tyrant opined from behind me.

"Huh?" I replied, my hands holding my shirt up as I tilted my head back to look at him.

"Ridiculous. Why do you drop your pants like that? Ha ha ha," he chuckled at me, then pointed and sneered as another man walked by. The other man chuckled too.

"I dunno," I said. My face was becoming hot and it was difficult to pee.

"No one wants to see your tush, Zach. Ha ha," he said, then walked up to urinal next to me and began doing his business.

I finished and walked up to the sink to wash my hands. I avoided eye contact with the men in the room. My face was still hot. The swap meet used the same harsh, pink soap the school and doctor's office used. I hated it but knew I had to wash after. The Tyrant shook his hands dry after barely washing them, then used his elbow to open the door back to the main building. He seemed to be strutting. *I really hate you,* I thought as I thoroughly washed my hands with the pink soap. Then I walked out to the main building too.

The Tyrant and his friend were sipping coffee next to each other, their backs against the wall like always, chatting a little, and glancing around. Mom and Sarah sat across from them. I had nowhere to sit.

"Here's some quarters. Go play pinball," Mom said with an apologetic smile.

I took the quarters and marched over to the machine. A woman named Elvira was featured in the picture above the glass. She appeared to be a demonic woman of some kind, with massive, jet black hair, tight black clothes, pale skin... and enormous breasts, which were pressed together in her tight black outfit. I contemplated her for a moment, then started playing.

I was never good at pinball and today was no exception. Haphazardly pressing the buttons on the side, often too early or too late, I kept losing and was running low on quarters. Elvira kept catching my eye though, every time the ball was launched and went up towards her picture. I was on my last set of quarters when it happened.

Pulling the plunger out and releasing, the ball traveling up and around, I looked up at Elvira one more time. Suddenly, my crotch began inflating. I hadn't felt that since French Greetings at recess. My heart started to pound and my face, finally feeling normal after the Tyrant's mocking, became hot again. The ball traveled down, hit two bumpers, and then went past the pedals. I didn't bother to push them. My hands dropped to my side and a small series of coughs escaped from my mouth. Something in my chest rolled over. I moved my hands to cover my crotch and ran to the men's room, then into a stall, locking the door behind me.

I frantically unbuttoned and unzipped my pants, then pulled the waistband of my whitey tighties out and looked at what was happening to me. *Why is my wiener doing this?* It didn't look like it was mine anymore. *What's wrong?* My eyes filled with tears and I started to sniffle. Then the men's room door opened.

"Zach?" It was the Tyrant's voice.

"Zach, you in here?" he asked.

"Yeah," I murmured.

"Why?"

69

"I… I don't feel good."

"Well, finish up. We're heading home. Wouldn't want to leave you behind." He said the last part sarcastically as he walked away. I heard the men's room door swing closed. It was a usual trick of his. He knew from Mom that I was afraid of being left behind.

I zipped up and buttoned my pants in a hurry and ran out of the bathroom, tears spilling down my face now. And there was Mom, my only source of warmth in times like that.

"Oh, Zach, what's wrong?" She asked in that motherly tone of hers.

"He feels sick or something," the Tyrant answered for me. I nodded my head at Mom.

"Come here. It's okay," she said.

The Tyrant shook hands with his friend, picked up his prize, and we walked back to the Taurus and drove home. As I sat in the car, munching on a stale poppy seed muffin, I told myself, *I'm never going to be like him. I'm never going to make people feel as bad as he does. I'm never going to like doing that.*

12

Open House

Location: Maple Valley, WA
Age: 9

The Tyrant made us a dining room table. He was rather capable at woodworking. I spent a lot of time at that table, either eating or doing my homework. I wasn't allowed to do my homework in my bedroom anymore, because I lied about it once.

The front door opened, and the Tyrant walked in, home from work. I looked at the clock. It was 5:30 P.M. *A little late. Traffic must have been slow. He's probably in a bad mood.*

I stood up from the table and my math homework. "Hello. How was your day?" I asked.

"It was alright. Traffic was a pain," he replied. Mom turned from the beef stew she was making in the kitchen.

"Hi, honey," she said. They embraced, and he kissed her with that mustache of his. I was never comfortable seeing that.

"What's for dinner?" he asked.

"Just some stew. We've got the open house at Rock Creek tonight."

"That's right," he turned from her towards the cabinet and his gin.

I resumed my math homework. The freezer door opened, and I heard his hand grasping around the ice, grabbing a couple cubes, and dropping them in his glass. Then the sound of carbonation escaping as he twisted the top off the tonic water and started to pour. He walked to the living room and pressed some buttons. Garth Brooks started playing.

Blame it all on my roots, I showed up in boots, and ruined your black-tie affair…

I sighed, and Mom glared at me. She raised her eyebrows. I looked down at my homework. It was hard enough hearing country music so often, but he always started with the same song too.

I was in advanced math, but still had to do the normal homework on top of it, which was easy but time-consuming. With multiplication tables, I could do it in my head, and the Tyrant didn't like this. He believed very strongly in showing your work.

"What'cha working on?" he asked, standing next to me, looking over my shoulder.

"Just some math homework. I wanted to get it done before dinner."

"What did we talk about?" he asked.

"Huh?"

"Didn't we talk about showing your work?"

"Oh, yeah. But these ones are just multiply by ten. Anyone can add a zero."

"So, you think you can just do it all in your head?" he sounded angry. *Traffic must have been bad.* And his office job was in a dying occupation. He said so himself once.

"No. That's not what I meant. It's just when it's only by ten, it's pretty simple. Anything times ten... you just add a zero to the other number."

"Mmmhmph."

"What?"

"Do it again," he instructed.

"But it's just by ten."

"AND I SAID DO IT AGAIN!" he snatched the paper out from under my hand.

"Here. Take a new piece of paper," he said, pulling my notebook out from my backpack on the chair, "And write all the problems down. AND. SHOW. YOUR. WORK. I won't tell you again."

"Okay. Okay." I pulled a paper from the spiral and placed it on the table. I started to write the problems out. His hands dropped to his side.

"WHAT DID WE TALK ABOUT?"

"What?"

"LOOK AT WHAT YOU'RE DOING TO THE TABLE. DO YOU SEE THE IMPRINTS IN THE WOOD? ALWAYS PUT A SHEET UNDERNEATH!" he slapped me in the back of the head.

"Okay. Okay. I'm sorry." I did as I was told. I looked Mom's way. She was looking at me, then made a sad smile and turned her head towards the little TV over the stove. She raised the remote control and clicked the volume up.

"DON'T LOOK AT HER!" he yelled.

"Okay. Okay."

"You think this is bad? My dad hit me with a frying pan. Now show your work and don't press so hard on the table. I won't tell you again." He exhaled loudly and stormed off to the garage. I felt someone's eyes on me and side-eyed the staircase. Sarah was peering over the railing, watching but not wanting him to notice her.

I couldn't focus for a moment, but slowly restarted my homework, making sure to show all my work. A few Garth Brooks songs played. The Tyrant returned to make himself another drink, stopping to look over my shoulder for a moment after. It always seemed like he was just about to hit me.

A few minutes later, dinner was served, and I packed my homework away. We had beef stew with carrots, potatoes, and biscuits. I was exhausted and rested my arm on the table. A stabbing sensation occurred in my elbow and I pulled away.

"Mmmhmmph," The Tyrant said as he pulled his fork away from my arm. Resting my arms on the table was something else he had spoken to me about.

"How was everyone's day?" he asked with a big, dumb smile.

"Mine was okay. We painted animals from the rainforest," Sarah said. The Tyrant looked at me. I could feel it.

"Mine was fine."

"Look at me when you answer," he said.

"Mine was fine," I said as I stared at him. He dropped his utensils on the plate.

"You got some attitude?" he raised his eyebrows.

"No. My day was fine though." *Why does he hate me?*

Before anything else could happen, Mom chimed in. "Work was fine, but I got a little burn on a tray of pizza. Lunch was hectic. It's always hectic on pizza day."

"Your hand okay, honey?" he said in a sympathetic tone.

"Yeah, it was just a little burn."

We finished eating, then got in the Taurus and drove to Rock Creek for the open house. The Tyrant drove, with a red party cup in the holder in the center console. There was a smooshed slice of lime in it, amongst the ice and gin. We listened to "Kickin Country K106" on the radio. Garth Brooks came on again. I imagined Garth was a nice man and I shouldn't hold his music against him. But I couldn't help but hate him too.

"Where should we go first?" Mom asked Sarah and I as we entered Rock Creek. I looked at Sarah. She looked back. I knew I had good grades and she didn't. Mine were all "+" but she had a few "-," which the Tyrant thought was "basically an F." He would spank us if we got bad grades.

"How about the library?" I said.

"Yeah! The library!" Sarah said.

"Okay," Mom replied.

"Just not too long. We need to see your teachers," the Tyrant declared. He had a slight smile on his face. The mustache was raised a little at the ends.

I made a beeline to the library with Sarah close behind. We split up inside as she headed for the books she liked, and I made way to the castle section. I thought I might bump into my friend John there, since he liked castles too. His parents were the only self-declared Democrats that I knew back then, and they both despised the Tyrant. They even stopped going on camping trips with us because of him. I think the final straw was when he spanked Sarah repeatedly in front of them. Sometimes I walked to their house to play with John. Other times I went just to get away.

I was almost to the castle books when I heard footsteps behind me. There was a gentle shove to my shoulder. I thought it might be John, but it wasn't.

"So, you think your teacher is giving you good grades?" The Tyrant asked.

"Yeah. I have all plusses. I'm sure."

"Think you're so smart huh? I know you're not that smart."

"Yeah, I am. I'm in advanced math."

"Still need to show your work."

"It's only times ten," I remarked under my breath. He heard me though.

Suddenly I was traveling forward and falling, as he shoved me from behind. I bounced against a book cabinet, then hit my head on the corner of a second one.

"Owwww. Why?" I asked from the ground. I reached up to touch my head. He grabbed me and raised me to my feet. My hand found something on my head that hadn't been there since the car accident when I was almost four years old, back when Mom and Papa were still together.

There was something warm and sticky on my hand. I pulled it away from my head to look at it. I saw blood and started to cry. I wheezed. The Tyrant's face and mood instantly changed. He became like a child that is afraid of getting into trouble.

"Hey Deb!" he yelled across the library. Mom came over quickly.

"Oh my god, Zach! What happened?" she asked.

"We were horsing around, and he fell," The Tyrant answered for me. I wanted to say the truth, but I was overwhelmed and crying and having trouble breathing. So, I didn't.

"Okay well let's go. We need to go see the doctor," Mom said, trying to speak in a calm voice. Sarah walked over to see what was going on. Then she dropped her book and started crying.

We made our way to an Urgent Care, where I got three stitches. Weeks later, Mom and I drove over to the house of one of my friends from Cub Scouts. His mother, an RN, cut the stitches to remove them. She didn't charge.

13

The Long Grass

Location: Ocean Shores, WA (West of Seattle, along the
Pacific Coast)
Age: 11

The swap meet was a weekly occurrence during summer, but
the main event of the season was a family trip to Ocean
Shores for the 4th of July. We went every year, and after staying a
few other places, once even camping on the beach, we adopted the
Grey Gull as our getaway of choice.

The Grey Gull was a smaller hotel, with only three floors and a
main office in the middle. The building formed an obtuse angle,
though I originally thought it was right, whose arms pointed
towards the ocean, with the office as a vertex, and a pool with a
small hot tub on the ocean-side. The paint on the exterior of the
building was a faded blue-gray. On the second and third floors,
where some of my aunts and uncles stayed, there were small
balconies facing the ocean. We always stayed on the first floor

though, the furthest unit to the left if one faces the ocean, with a small deck and steps down to the grass and pebble stones leading to the pool.

The ocean was just a short walk away, over the dunes, the pathways in varying stages of cleared, solid sand beneath your feet, the occasional colony of ants marching to and fro, and long grass swaying in the salty air. Down on the beach there were kites flown by the visitors' children, sand dollars to collect, a tide to race in and chase out, and the occasional police vehicle pulling someone over. And then there were the fireworks in the evening, in such amounts that the air lost its salinity in favor of the egg-like smell of black powder.

The Tyrant drove, as he always did since he's the man, and we pulled into the covered offloading area next to the office. I carried some of the bags as we made our way to check-in, the kind clerk giving us the rundown of the place before realizing how often we'd been there. Then off to the room to drop our bags down and enjoy Kentucky Fried Chicken before it got cold. We always had K.F.C. the first night of our vacations.

We were only there a few days each year, so we made the most of it, and after meeting up with our relatives, we assembled our provisions and were off to the beach. I carried the newspapers, which we used to start our fires, and a few small bags of fireworks. The Tyrant carried some camping chairs on his first trip, then a small cooler on his second. Mom might carry a chair or some blankets, but she was mainly transporting Sarah. Sarah didn't like how windy the beach was and imagined she was suffocating whenever the wind hit her face. We were all in jean jackets or sweatshirts, covering the matching Old Navy American flag T-shirts Mom bought on sale for us each year to mark the occasion.

There was a nice flat area in the sand next to a large piece of driftwood. We setup our chairs there and I scurried off to collect wood for a fire. I was instructed to only collect the wood that was already dry. The fire started, and we sat in our chairs enjoying the warmth and watching the sun slowly descend towards the horizon. I drank a Cherry Coke while Mom and the Tyrant sipped from red party cups what was undoubtedly gin and tonic. Sarah sat in a chair far too large for her but didn't seem to mind. No fireworks yet from us; I wasn't permitted to light them until after it was dark. It wasn't quite night yet.

"I think we're out of tonic, sweetie," Mom said some time later, as she retrieved a plastic bottle from the cooler.

"There's more back at the place. I'll get it," The Tyrant replied. He took a gulp from his glass, then stood up and marched off, empty bottle in one hand and his drink in the other. I watched which pathway he took. I needed to pee, but it wasn't urgent enough yet for me to get up, and I wanted to make sure we didn't cross paths. I didn't like being alone with him.

I poked at the fire with a small stick, moving the coals around, then stacked a few pieces of driftwood on top to keep it going. "I'll be right back," I said as I got up.

"Where are you going?" Mom asked.

"I need to pee."

"Okay."

"I need to pee, too," Sarah said.

"Take your sister with you," Mom instructed.

"Fine," I sighed. Sarah smiled and hopped from her camping chair. We took the longer path back to our room. She tried to hold my hand.

"Stop it," I barked. She tried again.

"Sarah, knock it off!"

She giggled a bit, content to annoy me in whatever way she could. I suspected she didn't even need to use the bathroom, because that's how little sisters are.

"Be careful in the grass," I said to her as we walked into the dunes.

"Why?"

"Because there's raptors in the long grass. Remember? Oh yeah, you weren't allowed to watch it because you're too little."

"Watch what? What's a raptor?"

"A raptor is a dinosaur that cuts your stomach open with large claws. It hides in the grass."

She tried to hold my hand again, and I pulled away. She wasn't giggling anymore.

"Please?" she asked. I let her. Just so long as it was out of fear and not a desire to annoy me.

We were nearly back to the room when I saw the Tyrant emerge on the deck, lighting up a smoke before walking towards the path next to ours. He was easy to spot because he always wore the same camouflage baseball cap. I crouched down. Sarah copied.

"What is it?" Sarah asked anxiously.

"Shhhhhh!"

"Is it raptors?" She asked in a little voice.

"No. I just don't want him to see us," I whispered. Sarah raised her head above the grass.

"I don't like him either," she said, shaking her head.

"Yeah." I tugged her arm and she lowered herself again.

The Tyrant marched along his path, fresh bottle of tonic in one hand, and party cup in the other. He took a slurp from it as he approached on our left. I heard rotor blades reverberating in the distance. They got closer and closer.

The red and white U.S. Coast Guard helicopter flew directly over us, towards the ocean. I stood up to look at it, then glanced over to see if the Tyrant had seen me. He was now squatting low to the ground amongst the grass, looking all around, occasionally peering up to see where the helicopter went. The reverberations became lower as it traveled further away from us. The Tyrant raised his red party cup to his face and took a large gulp, then another, holding it with two shaky hands. The tonic bottle was on the ground, a lit cigarette next to it. Then I caught his eye and saw his fear.

He was a forgotten son of American militarism. I feared him and hated how he treated us, but even then, I knew it wasn't all his fault. The Man did it to him. And The Man told him not to talk about it. His original sin was that he listened.

We launched some small fireworks that night once it was dark. Then we packed up our things and headed back to the room. We always brought a few bags to collect the debris from our fireworks.

On family vacations we usually had two beds. Sarah and I would share one while Mom and the Tyrant took the other. We settled down for the evening and turned out the lights. It always took me a long time to fall asleep.

***

In the darkness, sometime later, I heard a slapping sound that was painfully familiar to me. I opened my eyes and looked towards the other bed. I could see Mom; she was facing my direction. She wasn't moving and seemed to be asleep. I rotated my head and looked at Sarah. She was also asleep and motionless, so far as I could tell. The slapping sound continued and increased in speed, just like the times I'd heard it before. I retreated into the covers.

"There it is," I heard the Tyrant whisper to himself as the slapping reached its fastest rate. I winced as I pulled the covers over my face and curled up in a ball. The slapping continued and then suddenly stopped. The Tyrant stifled a groan. Then I heard footsteps to the bathroom and toilet paper being pulled and the toilet being flushed. The Tyrant returned to his bed and went to sleep.

I peered out from the covers at the other bed again. Mom was as she was before. I felt very bad for her. I wondered what things she had to do since she slept with him. *Hopefully he's not like Uncle Bobby.*

The Tyrant started to snore, and more time passed. The digital clock was nearly to 1 A.M. the last time I saw it.

***

The next thing I remember is the sound of Sarah screaming and crying. She was on the floor next to our bed. The covers were all over the place. My heart was racing, and I couldn't breathe. The lights flipped on.

"What the hell?" The Tyrant said.

"Sarah? What's wrong honey?" Mom got out of bed and walked over.

"Zach kicked me out of the bed," Sarah said between sobs.

"Zach, why did you do that?" Mom asked.

"I hit the wall," Sarah whimpered.

"Answer your mother," The Tyrant instructed me. I took a deep breath, as deep as I could.

"I don't remember," was all I could say.

14

The Talk

Location: Maple Valley, WA
Age: 13

Mom always did the laundry. When I was 13, she discovered a towel with tell-tale signs that I had entered puberty. There was a gentle knock on my door and then she walked in, towel in hand. I turned from my math homework and was petrified by what I saw.

"We need to talk," she said. Mom was in her forties at this point and dyed her hair to keep it brown. We celebrated her 39th birthday every year. A few inches taller than the average woman, she stayed thin with SlimFast, and was always tan from sunbathing. She had friendly eyes and a forced, sad smile.

I had always wondered who was going to be the one to tell me about sex and condoms and the pill. I knew it wasn't going to be my dad, but I always assumed Mom and the Tyrant would just flip a coin or, my preference, punt and let the school tell me about it.

The thought of learning about sex in a room with other kids and the jokes we'd make and how serious the teacher would pretend to be sounded far better than an awkward talk at home. But here we were.

"First of all, we're going to get you some Kleenex and you're going to stop ruining towels. Do you think anyone wants to dry off with this even after it's been washed?"

"No…"

"Also, don't do *that* too much. It will mess with your mind and bend your dick." I had a brief flashback to another time she was concerned about my dick. *The doctor. She just sat there.*

"Do you want to know about sex?"

"I'm taking health class next year," I said and turned around, back to math.

"That's for learning about diseases and memorizing parts of genitals. You already know what sex is though right?"

I nodded at my desk and stared out the window. The boys and I had watched a porno together at Mikey's house. *Dollar and Yen.* It was the first time I ever watched porn and by far the most awkward. Knowing that your friends are all getting aroused the same time as you, and in such proximity, is a rather disconcerting feeling. The film was shut off when one of our Mormon friends found out what we were watching when we called for him to come over. Like a good Mormon, he told his mom and she then told Michael's mom. We hid the tape and lied to her. I eventually bought that film for $20 out of my accumulated allowance, and a few years later, flipped it for $60 from a guy on the swim team. Not a bad deal for either of us. It beat dial up.

"So, the school will fill you in on the parts and the risks and the church will tell you about the risks some more…" Mom had encouraged me to start going to youth group at the Presbyterian church in town. It made my grandmother happy, though the Alzheimer's was slowly making it so she didn't know much of anything, including how to be happy. I kept on at the church despite that because I had a few friends there and was crushing on a pretty brunette that was out of my league but nice about it. It also kept me away from the Tyrant and the church served tacos for dinner on Wednesdays.

"… but that's not all you need to know about sex, Zach."

"Church will tell me that I need to get married first. I'll follow that, and my wife and I will figure it out from there. Do you have any advice on how to have a happy marriage?" I squinted at her as I turned around.

Mom looked down and let the towel fall to her side. She stood there in silence for a moment, then continued, a melancholy tone to her voice now. "You need to know when it is and isn't okay to do something with a girl. I'm not talking just about getting married and just sex. I'm talking about kissing, touching, all that, before and after getting married. You need to
have permission first."

"Yeah, I know. Just because I jizzed on a towel doesn't mean I'm a rapist, Mom. The towel isn't a girl. It's a towel."

"Do you remember that I was a model before you were born?" She did modeling work in and around Seattle for several years when she was younger. It was the 1970s. I'd seen some of her old photos from back then. Beautiful. She made a good living at it, enough to support herself and travel a little, but she never took the next leg up and eventually moved on. She left Seattle to become a flight attendant in Hawaii. That's where she met a retired Air Force officer turned airline pilot who became her husband.

"Yeah, you did that before you met Papa."

"Do you know why I stopped modeling?"

"No."

"There was a boat party on Lake Washington. Me and some of the girls were invited by this photographer we knew. A few baseball players were there. A businessman from Bellevue owned the boat. Anyways," she sighed, "well, some men don't take no for an answer and I had to jump overboard and swim half-naked to shore."

I was stunned. After a moment, I managed, "Mom, I'm so sorry."

"I know. It wasn't you that did it. But you should know it wasn't the only time something like that happened. The photographer apologized and said the baseball guys just got too drunk and I wanted to believe him. I wanted to believe it was just some accident or something. So, I stayed in modeling, but then more things happened, and I got really sad and decided to leave."

"And that's how you met Papa?"

"Eventually. Yeah. But Zach I blamed myself for a long time. I thought I was stupid and that I should have known better."

"No no. They shouldn't have done that to you."

"I know that now, but I didn't when I was younger, and I hated myself for it. And a lot of the girls you know from school and then when you're off in college, you could probably get away with it like those guys did. A lot of them would probably hate themselves too. That's why you need to know how much I got hurt." Her eyes were full of tears, but the dam hadn't broken. She turned and walked out of the room and I heard the knob of the washer turn and it filled with water.

I started to feel bad about myself in a way I couldn't fully grasp back then. She had suspected Uncle Bobby was a molester, but never talked to me about it. Did she feel ashamed or was it not severe enough to count? Or had she just forgotten? I felt illegitimate.

15

Sexual Education

Location: Maple Valley, WA
Age: 14

The old junior high had three floors and was made of brick. There were dingy, orange carpets inside, rumored to be from the 70s. It was a relic of a school and smelled like Nana's old house in Seattle. The linoleum cafeteria floors had warps. My locker didn't open properly, and I quickly gave up on using it. Eighth grade was the best year of my life up to that point, though.

In the Tahoma School District back then the 8th graders were split between Glacier Park and the old junior high. The split was done by proximity, with a few exceptions. Glacier Park, with its bullies, was about a twenty-minute walk from my house, as I had learned in 7th grade when I had to quit riding the bus to avoid them. It was uphill both ways and a pain in the ass. And I would have gone to Glacier Park again in 8th grade had it not been for math class.

In 7th grade I took 9th grade math. In 8th grade I was to take 10th grade math and 10th grade math was only offered at the old junior high. It was the second time in my life that being a nerd paid off; the first time being the friends I made in 7th grade. I followed advanced math, and several of those new friends, to an old, brick refuge away from the bullies of Glacier Park.

It was strange riding the bus again and the trip was longer than I was used to. I didn't care though. I felt safe at school, even looked forward to going. My stepfather still went after me at home, but I was getting taller every year and lifted weights to make my arms larger. His abuse transitioned from the physically overpowering to verbally intimidating and then to verbally desperate. I could handle that, I thought. The 9th graders didn't like it when 8th graders hung out on the top floor before school, but if you avoided that floor, they treated you with indifference. That was fine by me.

I met a Polish/Algerian immigrant kid. He was quickly incorporated into the nerdy clique that formed the real foundation of my childhood. He introduced me to my favorite band of all time, Nirvana, though this was the late 90s, a couple years after Kurt Cobain's death. And we played soccer together on a non-competitive team, which was nice because I've never been good at soccer.

The most interesting thing I learned that year was how good it feels to be a nerd when nerdiness has no social consequence. The nerds and I flourished that year in the absence of our natural predators. We even acted up some, though nothing too bad.

I crushed on a couple girls that year and for the first time I got the strong impression that at least one of them liked me back. That boosted my self-esteem, though I was far too shy and awkward to ever do anything about it. The closest I got to finding a girlfriend was at school dances where a good friend or two would gently shove me towards a girl I liked, and she would smile and dance with me, neither of us speaking. That was a whole new world. I became hopeful that someday things might work out for me with a woman.

It wasn't all perfect though. Experience tends to remind. I couldn't escape my experiences and suffered intense bouts of depression and anxiety throughout the year. Somedays I would lay in bed after school or on the weekends all day, listening to Nirvana, feeling the things they felt, which seemed a lot like the things I had felt. Ditto Eminem, my second favorite back then. At my worst, I avoided girls at school because I thought I didn't deserve to be liked. They complimented me, especially my eyes, but I assumed it was all a lie.

I struggled to sleep, lying awake, imagining all the mistakes I could make and had made, internally bullying myself towards perfection. I would place my belongings against the bedroom door, barricading myself, so I would feel safe enough to sleep, even though no one was trying to hurt me anymore. I hid my BB gun between my bed and the wall, within reach should I ever need it.

At school, I still had an unrelenting urge to follow the rules and get perfect grades. The anxiety was the worst during passing periods, when I would imagine being late to class and how the teacher would be disappointed. If they got disappointed enough, I imagined, they might phone home and that would be the end of me. *The Tyrant is always looking for a reason to be mean.* I didn't know it then, but I was trying to survive. That's what it all boiled down to.

There was no strolling or lollygagging during passing periods for me. Each one was a death march from the class I had been in to the next class. I regularly arrived ahead of schedule, sometimes sweating. On occasion, I broke this routine, with horrible results.

The bell rang, and I got up from my desk in the 3rd row of a class whose subject I can't remember now. I waited as other students walked past me to the door, then began my journey to PE.

It was raining outside, the sky covered in menacing clouds. I approached the exit of the main building and checked my watch. There was still four minutes until the next period. *Ahead of schedule.* The gym was only about a minute away.

Some of my fellow Nirvana fans congregated by the main office between classes. I walked their way, confident I had time to spare. It was a motley crew of kids, some in black pleather pants, others in ripped jeans, some nerdy conformists like me, and others who refused to fit in. I can't remember all their names, but I remember what they looked like.

"So Neuhaus, when are you going to get a guitar man?" One of them asked me. He had red hair.

"As soon as I have the money. I've been looking at ads from Guitar Center," I replied.

"Fender?"

"I was looking at a Jackson actually. A Dinky is cheaper than everything other than the Squier. Something good to learn on since I don't know shit yet."

"Mmmmm. Yeah that's true." He nodded.

"Yeah."

"Well, when you do, we gotta make a band man. Two guitars and a drummer." It was a common refrain in 8th grade.

"Hell yeah," I concurred.

One of the girls handed me headphones and I put them on. She had dark hair and straps crisscrossing between her plaid pant legs. She held a CD player in her hands and pushed play. I knew the song as soon as it started. I smiled at her and nodded along.

Teenage angst has paid off well. Now I'm bored and old... man, I hope so. I hope this shit pays off. I chuckled.

The music blaring in my ears, I didn't hear the bell ring, but noticed as the group began dispersing. I took the headphones off.

"Shit, did the bell already ring?" I asked.

"Yeah, gotta go," plaid girl said as I handed her headphones back.

"See ya," I said as I started marching away.

"Later," a few of them replied.

I didn't want them to be reminded of how much I cared about school. I waited for them to exit my view and then started running.

The hallway alongside the gymnasium, where the locker room entrances were, smelled like stagnant air and dust, mixed with sporadic helpings of cleaning products and the sweat of generations of teens. I was reminded of body odor every time I entered.

I was surprised to find the locker room door locked and no noise emanating from the other side. *What the fuck?* The doors to the gymnasium were closed but unlocked. I entered. The gym itself was even more disgusting. The hallway aroma continued in there, accompanied by a thin film of grime on the floor and detritus hanging from large, caged warehouse lights overhead. The collective dust of these lights cast a yellowish hue in the room, like the unwiped lamps of habitual smokers. Like the orange carpets of the main building, these lights were relics of a bygone era. On occasion the supporting wires would tear on a light, causing it to hang ominously. Some fell, but no one was ever hit so far as I remember.

I stood in the gym for a moment bewildered and anxious. *Where the fuck is everyone?* And then it dawned on me: sex ed.

"FUCK!" I yelled in the empty gym as I turned and ran back to the main building.

Athletics were not my strong suit, I was a husky dude who ate too much, and was pushing my body to the limit to get to class. When I finally arrived at sex ed, I paused in the hallway to compose myself and wipe sweat from my forehead. Then I walked in.

"Sorry," I said meekly as the teacher paused his lecture and looked at me. A few classmates sniggered as I walked past them in search of an empty desk. I sat in the back, next to Vladimir, my Russian friend whom I'd started playing chess with the year before, in the Glacier Park library where we hid from bullies together. The teacher resumed the lesson, a diagram of a woman's reproductive organs projected onto the whiteboard.

"What's up?" Vlad whispered as I wiped more sweat from my forehead.

"I fucking forgot we had this today. I was in the gym," I whispered back. Vlad nodded.

The teacher gave a brief overview of the fallopian tubes and uterus and the rest of the organs. Whenever the word "vagina" was uttered there was the expected snickering and the teacher's stern, furrowed eyebrows. We were admonished to grow up, that this was not a joke.

Something happened to me when the teacher switched to the male anatomy. An image was projected of the penis and testicles, along with the assorted internal organs. The word "arousal" came up and one of the other boys whispered "boner." Everyone laughed. Except for me and the teacher, who continued, undeterred by adolescent immaturity.

"When the male is aroused, blood rushes to the penis, causing it to become hard and erect. In this state, it is able to penetrate the vagina. This is how vaginal sex occurs." The teacher said this matter-of-factly.

Another projection appeared on the whiteboard, this one a diagram of an erect penis. My sweat was different now, cold. My heart was racing more than it would have from running. I became dizzy.

"Dude…" I whispered.

"I don't like looking at dicks either," Vlad whispered back.

"No, I mean…" I blinked hard and trailed off. Vlad looked at me, then back at the whiteboard. I put my hands on my face. Everything seemed clammy.

Another projection, this one a side view of an erect penis with a small amount of fluid shooting from the tip. I heard heavy breathing from somewhere and my vision narrowed, taking on an orange hue on the periphery.

"Oh god," I said.

"Yeah!" one of the boys exclaimed.

"That's enough. You, out in the hall," the teacher dismissed the troublemaker.

The teacher turned his attention to me, turning his head sideways.

"Are you okay, Zach?" he asked. My vision was now a tunnel and I felt like I was about to die.

"No," I managed with a gulp. I don't know how loud I said it, but the teacher's eyes widened. My voice sounded like it was coming from another room.

"Okay. That's okay. Vladimir, why don't you walk Zach to the nurse?" Vlad got up and touched my arm. The heavy breathing continued. As we made our way up the aisle, I tried to not look at the erect penis in front of me.

Shaky, my legs like jelly, I staggered with Vlad to the hallway. He kept one hand on my arm and we worked our way down the orange carpet to the steps leading outside. The fresh air was cool on my head. I took a deep breath and sat down on the concrete steps. It was still raining. The heavy breathing faded to the pitter-patter on concrete.

"Oh man," I said, blinking, trying to force my vision back to normal. My legs shook like I drank too much soda.

"What's wrong?" Vlad asked.

"I don't know man. That just freaked me out for some reason," I confessed.

"Why can't you look at dick and pussy?" He asked.

"I dunno. I mean, I watch porn sometimes, but I dunno." I had no idea what was going on.

We sat out there for a while. I lowered my head to my knees and tried to think about video games and Star Wars cards. I'm not sure how much time passed, but by the time the bell rang, I was almost back to normal, aside from a headache that was taking over where the dizziness had left off. We walked back to health class to grab our things.

***

I didn't tell Mom about it at first. But then it happened again, the very next class. Apparently, I couldn't look at hard dicks without freaking out. This was confusing for me, as I was able to masturbate at home. I no longer experienced any anxiety about my own erections. Sometimes I would do it by myself, just my imagination. Other times I relied on visual aids like porn. In the one porno I had, there were dudes and they had sex with women. I didn't understand how I could see footage including those dicks and not freak out, but I did freak out when images of dicks were shown to me in class. I concluded that it probably had to do with not having a choice in the matter. *I didn't have a choice with Uncle Bobby and the others. I do have a choice with porn and my own imagination. A health class I'm required to be in, I've got no choice, no control.* I started to feel anxious about going to health class again, for fear of embarrassing myself further.

I was contemplating all of this when Papa rolled up to pick me up from school in his blue van that was dirty on the inside and clean on the outside. It was a Tuesday, one of his two weekly visitation days.

"Zachariah! How was school?" He asked while lighting a Winston Light 100. He had a beige jacket on and his big glasses.

"Terrible," I replied.

"What happened?" He asked in between drags. I thought better of telling him. *He wouldn't understand.*

"Oh… just too many tests is all," I lied.

"Did you do good on 'em though?" he asked, officially, peering at me through his bifocals. I could see some of his dandruff had collected on them.

"Yeah, I think so."

"Good." He put the van in drive and turned the radio up to a sports show. Sarah sat in the backseat poring over something in a black three-ring binder. It was my turn to sit up front.

We drove along for a while, him smoking and the men on the radio discussing stats. Then we approached the high school that I would attend two years later, and the national cemetery next to it.

"Oh, here we go," Papa said, excited.

"What?" I asked.

"Roll down your window," Papa said. I grabbed the handle and rotated it.

"Faster! Come on!" Papa ordered. He reduced speed as we approached. When we got next to the cemetery, Papa leaned towards me.

"SAVE ME A SPOT FELLAS!" Papa yelled out my window.

"… what?" I was bewildered.

"Heh heh heh," Papa chuckled.

I started laughing, too. *Oh, man.*

***

Later that evening, Papa dropped us off at the house in Maple Valley. I was stuffed from Mexican food and desperately needed to use the restroom. Mom stood by the staircase near the front door, like she'd been waiting for Sarah and me. My stomach made assertive noises at her.

95

"I've got some bad news," she said, placing her hands on our shoulders.

"What?" I asked. *What more could go wrong?*

"Bootsie died," Mom said. I must admit that for a moment I was thankful it wasn't my grandma or something. But then it sunk in and I started to feel sad.

"What happened?" Sarah asked.

"Well, I don't know for sure, but she's been gone all day and last night. I think she ran off to the woods behind the neighbors' houses."

"Oh. She's not dead then. She stays out late sometimes," I explained.

"No, honey, I'm sorry. She was acting kinda funny yesterday…"

"How so?" I demanded. My stomach uttered its own demands.

"Well, I was taking a nap on the couch and she came by meowing in this kitten type of tone. Then she hopped up on the couch and rubbed her face against mine for a while. Then she walked to the door and I let her out."

"And?"

"It's just how it felt. It felt different. She didn't really enjoy life anymore and was in pain. She was an old cat. She probably knew the end was near and went away to spare us all that. Some cats are like that." Mom frowned and rubbed our shoulders. Sarah hugged her, but I slipped away and walked upstairs to the bathroom to relieve myself and think.

16

Lost in Translation

Location: Maple Valley, WA
Age: 15

I got my first job when I was 14 years old. It was temporary, under-the-table landscaping work with a few friends the summer between 8th and 9th grade. Hard, miserable work. We hacked at endless blackberry bushes with dull machetes, dug holes, laid stones and bricks, and went home every day feeling dead. I hated it, but it paid.

Fast forward a little bit, and I'm 15 years old and need to find a job but don't want to do physical labor ever again. I applied to the two McDonald's in Maple Valley, and the one at Four Corners called me first, so I went with them.

For as long as I live, I will never forget the smell of McDonald's. You've smelt it too, anytime you drive by with the window down. It seems to be a combination of grease, salt, and other chemicals, added to heat and meat by people who don't want to be there. It doesn't smell exactly like the other fast food places. A distinct aroma. The first few times you come home with clothes that smell like it, you put the laundry hamper in the hallway to avoid contaminating your bedroom, but eventually it all seems normal and you stop noticing.

You learn things about people in your community by being a teenage cog in a bad food machine. People reveal their true personality to you when they think you're there to serve their whims. Like the middle-aged white women, the same age as your friends' parents, who go from zero to ten over pickles on their burgers and begin to scream like a belligerent child having a tantrum. And that tantrum is directed at you and the "Mexicans in the back. I mean, do they even speak English?" How could they know she definitely said that she can't have pickles on her burger? Even though she forgot to say any of it. Nothing is worse in life to her than pickles on a burger. It must be an odd feeling to be in a position of marginal power over others yet still feel dissatisfied with one's life. At least that's how I viewed them then. And their husbands, when they were there, stood silently, perhaps relieved that the outburst wasn't directed at them, quietly apologizing to me with reluctant stares.

My community seemed quite miserable.

I don't remember his name, but he was a skinny, white boy. Very skinny. And pale, almost so pale that there was a green tinge to him. Hollow eyes with dark circles under them; blonde hair parted in the middle, thinning prematurely. He was my shift supervisor at McDonald's. The other shift supervisor, who I only worked with on occasion, was his petite, mousy, girlfriend. They were both burnouts. I never knew for sure what they were on, but they were on something.

My suspicions were confirmed one day when I was working the drive-thru and he approached me with two large paper sacks of cheeseburgers and fries. They were nearly overflowing.

"Hey Zach, I need you to take a quick break," he said.

"No problem. I'm not sure what's going on with this customer though. They're pulling up to the window, but they haven't ordered anything." Their car was a poorly kept Honda Civic, with two dudes inside.

"It's alright. I know'em." He stepped past me and pulled two large cups and filled them with ice and Coca-Cola.

"Oh... okay," I said as I backed away, grateful for another break, but also suspicious. I was a Boy Scout, literally, and I attended church twice a week now. I really doubled down on conformity after the academics worked out on the home front. All this to say: I was uncomfortable with what I figured he was doing.

The car pulled up and the skinny white boy leaned far out the window, nearly off his feet. There was a small clap noise, a slap of the hands. Words were exchanged. He handed the overflowing bags down to the car and the drinks also. Then he leaned far out the window again and was handed a small brown bag. I was still standing by the drive-thru and his friend in the car noticed me through the window and nodded my way. Skinny boy turned around.

"Dude. I told you to take a break. Go!"

"Are they going to pay for that?"

"What? They already paid. What are you talking about?" He rolled up the brown paper bag to a small clump and shoved it in a front pocket in his faded black pants. His friends drove away.

"Really?" I asked.

"You know what? I think your break is over. I'll have someone else run the drive-thru. The cooks are short-staffed. Head back there and help out."

He exiled me to the grill and assembly area. My Food Handler's Permit was supposed to be a formality. My job was to run a cash register, hand out orders, apologetically survive being berated by customers, and maybe clean the lobby. I wasn't supposed to actually cook, unless dropping fries in oil counts.

I wandered back to the cooks. I didn't know them well, having only spoken to them briefly to ask for my shift meals, always a double cheeseburger with Big Mac sauce.

"Hello Zach," one of them said. The oldest one, with deep lines on his forehead and sad brown eyes.

"Hello. I'm supposed to work back here now."

"Oh, ha ha," he laughed. "He is punishing you!" More laughter followed by a few words in Spanish that he said to the others. They laughed too.

"Yeah, I guess so," I replied with a fake smile.

"Okay, gloves are over here," he pointed. "Wash your hands first."

It was hot back there with a steady sizzle of frozen beef patties on a flat top. There were little plastic drawers full of ingredients and wrapping papers under the shiny metal table. Spanish was spoken, except when they needed something from me, then they might say a few words in English. Otherwise, I just kept to myself and worked as fast as I could. They seemed to like me, though I could never keep up with them. The remainder of my McDonald's career was spent back there.

***

One day, when my teenage angst was more elevated than usual, I decided to try and mimic the two celebrities I liked the most: Eminem and the late Kurt Cobain. I didn't know exactly which one I was trying to impersonate more when I bleached my hair. I just know I didn't look like either of them afterwards and felt self-conscious about it.

I walked in to start my shift at McDonald's that day. Through the dining area, then to the cash registers.

"Nice hair man," Skinny white boy said, mockingly.

"Are YOU really going to make fun of how I look?" I replied. "Really? Are you high?"

"Go clock in," he dismissed me, rolling his eyes and shaking his head as I passed.

I walked back to the heat, the sizzle and Spanish now familiar to me. One of the cooks saw me and grinned.

"OH! Shakira!" He exclaimed. Another cook emerged from the breakroom.

"No no no," the second one said. "More like... ZACH'IRA!" They both erupted in laughter.

Fuck my life. Frowning, I washed my hands, put on gloves, and looked at the order screen, trying to tune everyone out, as they pointed and laughed.

It got busy that evening. It always did at some point. And I lost myself in the flurry of orders and heat and everyone around me moving fast. I forgot about my hair.

I was working next to Juan near the end of it. He had a thick mustache and was the only guy in the store bigger than me. There was something strange about one of his eyes. It was glassy in a way the other one wasn't, and the brown coloring was distorted. I noticed it whenever he said something to me, like "remember, no pickles, Zach'ira." He laughed a lot and whenever it was at my expense, he would touch my shoulder, to let me know he was only kidding around.

When things died down a bit that night, skinny boy sent most of us to the breakroom. I sat down at one of the tables, sipping a Mr. Pibb. My feet hurt a little and I flexed and stretched them in my black shoes. Juan and the old cook with sad eyes were speaking in Spanish amongst themselves, with a younger girl sitting quietly next to them. I had been noticing her for weeks now. She was very pretty but didn't say much. I couldn't tell if she was barely a kid or barely an adult. I pretended she was about my age.

The conversation between Juan and the old cook sounded serious and they kept glancing over at me. I remembered my hair and mentally prepared myself to leave if they came up with a new way to make fun of me.

"Zach," the old cook said.

"Yes?" I replied.

"Zach. Do you…" he gestured with his right hand but trailed off and started to look uncomfortable. He and Juan exchanged a few more words in Spanish.

"Do I what?"

"Do you like?" he asked, finally, pointing at the pretty girl, who was now looking at me, her beautiful dark brown eyes and perfect eyebrows reading like an indictment.

Oh no. They must have seen me looking at her.

"What?" I replied, flustered, my face heating up. More words in Spanish between Juan and the old cook with sad eyes.

"Do you like… girl?" the old cook asked, pointing again at the girl, who was now looking down, embarrassed.

"Oh no. No, I do not. It's okay." And then I got up and left the breakroom. I returned to the assembly area and leaned against the grill, burning my hand.

"Fuck!" I jumped up. I squinted at the order screen and saw a few burgers listed, so I started working again. Scooping burgers off the grill and onto buns, adding the condiments and everything else, and rolling them up in the wrapping papers, I passed the time.

A few minutes later the cooks rejoined me in the assembly area. They avoided eye contact with me as they washed their hands and got in position. Skinny white boy peeked his head in from the cash registers.

"Hey, we're really slow right now. Any of you want to go home early?" He asked.

I raised my hand. "Yeah, if I could that would be great." None of the other cooks raised their hands. They never wanted to go home early.

"Okay. You two clock out." He pointed at the old cook with sad eyes and the pretty girl. I frowned. He sneered then turned back to the registers. *Fuck this guy.* I fantasized about grabbing him by the feet and flipping him through the drive-thru window the next time his dealer drove by.

Pretty girl and old cook did as they were told, meandering to the till to clock out.

"Bye, Zach," the girl said, meekly, as she passed.

"Good night," I replied. I had the sneaking suspicion that something had been lost in translation.

"It's okay, Zach'ira," Juan chimed in. "Not much time until close."

"Yeah. Sure," I replied.

Around 8 o'clock there was a surge of orders from the lobby and a few from the drive-thru.

"Here we go, Zach'ira," Juan said while pointing at the order screen, now full. We worked fast, burger after burger, to complete all the orders. Juan started to sing. He'd never done that before.

Oh baby, baby, how was I supposed to know? He sang when skinny white boy told us we messed up an order.

And then, while looking at the order screen as new orders populated, *Hit me baby one more time*, and Juan pointed at the screen. He was speaking more English than I expected and was much louder now that the other cooks had gone home. I had a foreboding feeling as to why that was.

Juan and I frantically wrapped up the burgers for a large order, placed the bad food in bags and left them for pickup by skinny boy. Then there was an unexpected napkin on my forehead.

"Oh, Zach'ira. So tired," Juan said, wiping sweat off my forehead.

"What? Dude..." as I pulled my head away. I stared at him for a second with narrowed eyes.

More orders piled in. It was time for nuggets and N'sync.

"Chicken nuggets, Zach'ira!" Juan exclaimed.

"I really don't like Zach'ira," I replied. Juan made a faux frown.

We placed the nuggets in their box and placed them for pickup. Then more burgers, Big-Macs this time, with the annoying third bun in the middle. Then more nuggets. Then, just like that, no more customers. Dead.

It's tearing up my heart, when I'm with you... ZACH'IRA! Juan sang. Skinny white boy snickered at me from the front.

"What the hell, Juan?" I demanded.

"Oh, ZACH'IRA ZACH'IRA!" Juan replied.

"You two watch the front. I gotta piss," skinny boy said, smirking at me with raised eyebrows. Accusing me.

Dammit.

Just as skinny white boy exited our field of view, my suspicions were confirmed, and I was in a terrible place to deal with them. I was furthest back in the assembly area, standing in a corner. The grill was behind me, sizzling with a few patties. Pickup to my left. Assembly table in front. Only one way out, to my right, past Juan. It was then that he decided to make his move.

"KISS ME ZACH!" Juan yelled, enthusiastically, as he stepped towards me. I recoiled in fear.

"Dude, no. What the fuck?"

"KISS ME! KISS ME ZACH!" Juan continued to move in. I stepped forward and shoved him. He stumbled back and steadied himself.

"OH ZACH'IRA! KISS ME!" He started approaching again. I don't know if it was the double cheeseburger I had for my shift meal or Juan's advances, but my heart was pounding.

"JUAN! NO!" I yelled at him. He was startled but undeterred.

"OH ZACH! OH! KISS ME ZACH!" He yelled, taking another step my way, puckering his lips.

"Juan... I said no," I stated firmly. Juan bit his lower lip and stared at me. His hand drifted down to his crotch and took hold of it.

Terrified, I tried to scramble through the pickup window, jumping up and trying to slide through like a paper bag. I felt Juan's hand on my foot and I kicked at him. My foot made contact and I heard an "oomph" noise.

It was in this predicament that skinny white boy returned. He laughed, then said "Okay you two. No more fooling around back there." Juan relented. I slid past him. I walked to the till and, without permission, clocked out.

"Where do you think you're going... ZACH'IRA?" skinny white boy asked.

"I'm going home. I don't care," I replied, walking away. I stopped and turned. "AND WE WEREN'T FOOLING AROUND YOU FUCKING ASSHOLE!"

***

I told no one, aside from a friend at school, not a particularly close one. We were discussing Nirvana, which album was the best, all that, while sitting on a table in a courtyard at the high school. And then I said, "Man, fuck Kurt Cobain."

"Uhhhh what?" he replied.

"I'm glad he's dead. That fucker nearly got me raped. Fuck Eminem, too."

"Ummmm... what?" he replied.

"Dude, I'm never copying a celebrity's hair again. Right when I go blonde, this big dude tried to get at me when I was cornered by the grill."

105

He hesitated, then laughed. "No way man. Really?" He laughed some more.

"Yeah. I'm gonna quit that job. I'll go work at the Taco Bell/K.F.C. up the street or something. My friend, John, works there."

There was a pause in the conversation.

"Well, can you blame him? I mean… the bleach does kind of make you look like a little f*ggot." More laughter.

I sighed, pretended to laugh along, and told no one else.

***

I did quit the job though. No two-weeks' notice, no notice at all. No one had ever given me notice, *so why should I?*

Eight o'clock rolled around and I clocked myself out at the till. I didn't clean or restock or do anything I was supposed to do before leaving. Just clocked out and walked.

And on my way out, I saw Juan. He was standing in the lobby, surrounded by wrinkly white people. They were holding hands in a circle around him. Juan was looking at the ground while they prayed for him, a small stream of tears rolling down from his normal eye.

Good. Fuck that guy. That was my first thought.

But the next day, when I went past the McDonald's on the way to school, I couldn't help but feel a mix of anger and pity for Juan. I imagined his life was a sad, desperate one.

17

National Lampoon

Location: Greater Seattle Area & Spokane, WA
(Eastern WA)
Age: 16

I was 16 when I first had the confidence to pursue a girl.
    She was a year older than me and we met on the high school
debate team. Debate team was one of the many extracurricular
activities I filled my days with. There was math team, where I was
vice president; debate team, where I would be president the
following year; student government; youth group at church; boy
scouts, where I was the senior patrol leader; swim team; a part time
job at McDonald's (and later, K.F.C./Taco Bell); soccer; National
Honor Society; and the city youth council, where I typically
napped. I had a full slate of A.P. classes, had already received a
good score on the S.A.T., and did basically anything I could to
avoid home. I was a perfectionist about my grades. It was the best

way to avoid being harmed or criticized by my stepfather, unless I went too far and acted like I was "better" than him.

Cathy and I first got to know each other at a debate tournament at Thomas Jefferson High School. She did individual expository events while I focused on debate. I had started in Cross Examination debate but switched to Lincoln Douglas. The structure of the arguments was more satisfying, with less of an emphasis on talking quickly, like in Cross Ex. Cross Ex debaters were notorious for talking as fast as possible, with no care given to connecting with an audience or allowing an opponent to understand what was being said. It was a shallow, firehose type of debate where the goal was simply to win on technicalities when your opponent failed to identify an argument since you talked faster than they could write. There was no emphasis on lofty rhetoric or philosophy. I hated it instantly.

Cathy came by one of my debate rounds at Thomas Jefferson High and watched the entire thing. We spoke briefly after the round, which I won. She asked if she could come to the next round and I gave permission, though she didn't need it. Each round was open to all participants of the tournament, so long as they sat quietly and didn't signal anything to the debaters. She came along for that round and a few more that day. She seemed to like watching me debate.

After the tournament was over, we sat by each other on the bus ride home. I was nervous at first, as I was entirely inexperienced, save for a very brief make out on a park bench a year ago with a girl from church. I could tell Cathy was attracted to me by the tone of her voice and how she looked at me. I'd been told that girls playing with their hair while talking to you was a sign they liked you. She did that. She also asked me if I had a girlfriend already, another sure sign. Nothing came of it on the bus ride home, but she asked intently if I was going on the overnight trip to Gonzaga a few weeks later. I'd signed up. Spending a weekend away from home at a debate tournament sounded fun and I had a National Lampoon type fantasy about what it would be like when the debate team stayed overnight in a hotel. Mr. Williams, a kind, patient man who was our coach, and the adult volunteers, would likely be incapable of preventing most of our antics. Cathy and I agreed to hangout on the trip.

***

A few weeks passed. Cathy and I bumped into each other in the halls a few times at school. Brief encounters between classes. Friendly. Familiar. She still looked at me the same way and played with her hair.

The day finally came for us to get on the bus and head over to Spokane for the weekend tournament at Gonzaga. I got on the bus and sat down next to Cathy. She was frowning and her hair had no volume.

"What's wrong?" I asked.

"I had to have surgery on my ovary. There was a cyst. I'm sorry."

Apparently, she had been reading into the situation even more than I had. I imagined maybe I would get a hand job or something. I had not expected to lose my virginity that weekend.

"That's okay. I wasn't expecting you to sleep with me. You don't owe me anything."

She kissed me on the cheek, and no longer seemed sad.

We sat like that, on the bus together, talking a little, and sharing a CD player with Nirvana's *Incesticide* playing.

We got to Spokane and checked into our hotel. I was going to be sharing a room with my buzz cut friend Colby, who promptly left to get food. I wasn't hungry. I heard some commotion in the hallway as Colby left. I stepped out to see what the matter was. Mr. Williams and a few parents were walking quickly down the hallway going away from me. "Some students already escaped!" Colby said with glee. About six of them had left the hotel as soon as they checked in and made way to an old abandoned church. They were goth or emo or whatever. I didn't spend time with people who wore all black and always looked pale. They seemed sickly to me and their attitudes sucked. Later, I decided they were pretty cool, after I got to know them. The adults all left the building in search of those moody white kids in black.

I went back into my room and closed the door. Then there was a knock. I knew it wasn't Colby. I opened the door and Cathy walked in. We immediately embraced and kissed. Her mouth tasted like spearmint gum. We made our way to the bed. It was difficult for me to walk. I was wearing jeans and had a throbbing erection. I don't think I'd ever been that hard.

Once on the bed, I reached for her pants, even though I knew Jesus wouldn't approve. I got halfway down from the waistline before I remembered her surgery. I pulled my hand out. "Sorry, I forgot." She hadn't stopped me, but I thought if I proceeded, it might hurt her. I didn't know much about the female body and knew even less about cysts and how involved the work was to remove them. I just knew she said she had surgery and it involved her genitals and I remembered how much it hurt when my skin got ripped. And how much it stung to move the skin after. She smiled and reached her hand over to my pants and undid the top button, then unzipped the zipper. My cock was sticking out of the top of my smiley-face boxers. I saw her eyes widen as she took hold of my cock with her hand. Her eyes glimmered up at me as she grinned. "It's really hard," she said. I couldn't say anything in response. I just stared back at her.

She pulled my cock all the way out of my boxers and started to stroke it. I became dizzy. I felt cold sweat forming on my forehead. *Fuck my life, really?* Her smile faded to concern, and I looked away, at the white popcorn ceiling above. My cock went limp. She didn't give up though and kept working it with one hand and then the other.

I said nothing and then a butterfly fluttered its wings in my chest, and I passed out, at least I think I did.

The story resumes for me seven-ish minutes later, according to the digital clock next to the bed. My cock is hard again... and wet.

"Oh my God," I said. Her smile was back, and she was looking in my eyes, her hand working below. I don't know how it got wet.

"I've seen *American Pie*. I know guys get nervous. Just relax," she said with a smile.

I knew the scene she was referring to. I knew that wasn't what had just happened. The cold sweat had made my hair slick and I could feel a trickle slowly run down my cheek by my ear. My heart was racing and fluttering a bit still. She stroked more rapidly now. My legs were tingling like they'd fallen asleep. The moisture allowed her to finish me off. My legs tensed and stretched out. My cock felt harder. Detecting the end was near, she said "cum for me," and I did. It was overwhelming. It shot all the way up to my chin and nearly got in my mouth. She giggled. I grabbed her hand to stop the motion.

"Holy shit, that nearly went in my mouth," I said.

She giggled again and went to the bathroom to wash her hand. When she returned, I got up to go fetch a towel in the bathroom. She tilted her head with worried eyebrows as I walked by, the smile had faded from her face again. I got in the bathroom, closed the door, and began cleaning my shirt and pelvis area of the semen. I wiped my chin with a small washcloth. As I looked up into the mirror to make sure I got all of it, I realized I was crying.

18

Boy Scouts

Location: Camp Parsons (West of Seattle on Hood Canal)
Age: 16

The Tyrant forced me to join Cub Scouts when I was in elementary school. I hated this at first, but eventually came to love scouting, and stuck with it the rest of my childhood. I got my *Arrow of Light* to finish Cub Scouts, then immediately crossed over to a Boy Scout troop.

The biggest difference I experienced with Boy Scouts was going to summer camp every year. In Cub Scouts there were programs like "Mom and Me" camp, where you'd go camping with your mother and everyone else's mothers. It wasn't typical to spend a long time away from your family. In Boy Scouts this was different. Though there were adult leaders on every campout, my mother never went, and eventually the Tyrant didn't either.

My first summer at Camp Parsons, I cried a lot. That was unexpected. I was basically inconsolable. I think it's because I felt abandoned, not being by my mother for a week. That changed with time. Camp Parsons became THE thing I looked forward to every summer. It's a beautiful camp out on Hood Canal, with tons of trees, a pier out into the ocean, friendly staff, a dining hall and trading post, and all the merit badges you could want.

In my early years at Parsons, the canoe swamp was my favorite thing. Everyone in the troop gets into shiny silver canoes, three or four boys a piece, and paddles out into the water along the pier. There are no oars, so you're just using your hands. Once everyone is situated, the canoe swamp begins. The goal is to sink other canoes and not be sunk. Your crew, typically boys of a similar age from your patrol, paddles over to another canoe, grabs the sides of it, and begins shoving down and pulling up until the rhythm causes the other canoe to fill with water.

The older boys, high school juniors and seniors, were at an obvious advantage due to size and strength. It was a rite of passage to be targeted and sunk by their canoe. I remember the first time I went under. One of my crewmates had an older brother, who was for my money the strongest in our troop at that time. His canoe came right at us, with a speed that seemed motor powered rather than from hand paddling. They gripped the side of our canoe and we tried to fight them off. But no matter how much we pushed on their canoe, it would barely budge. And every time they shoved, our canoe acted like it was about to go to the bottom. Three or four thrusts was all it took for them to sink us. We descended into cold saltwater.

Camp staff had instructed us on what to do next. How to move your canoe to shallow water or shore. How to pick it up as a team and get the water out of it. How to climb in without sinking. But you don't always remember your training when you're in cold, saltwater, with a crewmate who just remembered his fear of crabs. Crabs that are definitely lurking below. And so we panicked. And the older boys saw. And rather than mocking us or leaving us or lecturing us, they stopped what they were doing and helped. A scout is supposed to be Helpful after all.

Two of the older boys got out of their canoe and helped us carry ours to shallow water. Then they showed us, much the same way camp staff had, how to pick up the canoe as a team, flip it, and then flip it again and climb inside. It was then that I knew I could trust the Boy Scouts. No one was trying to hurt me. This was just a game.

***

Time went by and eventually I became one of the older boys. My patrol would target the other canoes and sink them, then stick around to make sure they were alright. Canoe swamp was no longer my favorite activity at that point. The boys and I were up to something else.

When Boy Scouts commit mischief it barely counts as "trouble" in wider society. We never did anything crazy.

We did sneak out a lot at night though. Sometimes a green-haired musician, with a kind-heart and affinity for chalk-based artwork, would lead us out to the pier where we would draw for hours, until the boards were almost all covered with chalk. Other times we'd sneak into the dining hall and remove the banners of other troops. We threw toilet paper and shaving cream filled water balloons at other campsites. On occasion, we temporarily stole their duty rosters as well.

It was good, clean fun. No one got hurt and, aside from the water balloons, we used biodegradable materials too. We were technically breaking a bunch of rules, but didn't care, and the adult leaders for our troop were generally indifferent to it. A few of them even took an interest in assisting us.

My second to last year at camp, we got very serious about these "covert operations" we were conducting. I was the senior patrol leader then and had to approve all covert actions. Someone else came up with the idea to paint our faces green and brown and black so we could better avoid detection. I thought it was a good idea.

It was late one of those nights, after chalking the pier, that I stood in our campground bathroom trying to remove face paint with cold water. My co-conspirators had already gone to bed for the most part. The green-haired musician was still at the pier, applying his finishing touches.

I splashed cold water on my face again and rubbed with a white towel. The running water made me feel like taking a leak, so I stopped and walked over to a urinal.

I heard footsteps alongside the bathroom wall. Heavy footsteps. They made way to the entrance and stopped by the sink. I turned my head and saw one of our adult leaders, Mr. Jackson, standing under the dim, yellow light bulb.

"Good evening, Zach," he said. He was a heavyset man with a beard. He went on all our campouts.

"Hey," I replied, then turned back to my urination.

The footsteps resumed on the concrete floor, the thud of them combining with dirt scratching to-and-fro with each step. The steps got closer to me, but I thought nothing of it. I assumed he needed to use one of the toilets.

"Looks like ya got a handful of fun there," he said, standing behind me, peering over my shoulder. I was startled and it took a moment for my mind to register the comment. He reached over my shoulder. I slapped his hand away.

"What the fuck!?" I said to him as I paused my piss and clenched my fists.

"Sorry, Zach. Sorry," he said as he backed away. His eyebrows were up with wide eyes.

"What the fuck are you doing?" I asked.

"Sorry," he said again. Then backed out of the bathroom, stumbled, regained his footing, and walked back to his cabin.

I immediately considered that it must have been a misunderstanding. I told myself not to think about it, that maybe it was some stupid joke or something. *Some of the adult leaders bring beer on these things. I bet he was loaded and just messing around.*

I tried to sleep that night, but really couldn't. I was too amped. There are no doors on the cabins. I kept imagining someone in the doorway as I tossed and turned in my sleeping bag.

***

Morning came and I heard Mr. Friday singing. He sang every morning about his three favorite things in the world: God, cars, and waking up scouts in the morning.

OH LORD, WON'T YA BUY ME, A BRAND NEW CAR? OH LORD, WON'T YA BUY ME, A MERCEDES BENZ? he sang. There were other songs or parts of songs, too. It always made me smile a little, even when my patrol was the one being subjected to it. I was groggy, but thought the day was going to be a good one.

I brushed my teeth and put on my class B uniform. The class B was a T-shirt with a scout saluting on the front. We wore it certain days. I liked it a lot because I could wear gym shorts with it.

After getting dressed, I called troop assembly. We raised the flag in camp and took roll. Everyone was present, except for Mr. Jackson. One of the adults walked over to his cabin. Mr. Jackson emerged a moment later, disheveled.

"Go on without me. I'll meet ya there," he said while walking to the bathroom. I led the troop out of our campground.

Before breakfast there is a camp-wide raising of the colors, followed by roll call. Every troop number is called and the senior patrol leader steps forward, salutes, and then says their troop number and "All present, sir" or "all accounted for" or "missing." I never heard "missing" in all my years at Parsons, but "all accounted for" was used when someone was sick back at camp, for example.

I led my troop to the grass field in front of the dining hall. The sky was clear blue. I gazed up and saw a bird flying close to the sun but couldn't make out what type it was. There was a soft breeze from the water behind us. We stood at attention and saluted as the flag went up. Then the director called roll.

"Troop 711?" the director announced.

I stepped forward.

"Troop 711, all present..." my gym shorts dropped to my ankles before I could say "sir." I was stunned for a moment, then covered myself and raised my shorts. I looked behind and saw Mr. Jackson, now in a scout uniform, scurrying back to the line of scouts. Mr. Friday and the other adults had mouths agape and eyebrows furrowed, like they were angry and surprised at the same time. I regained my composure.

"Troop 711, all present sir," I said with a salute. The camp director, also looking shocked, blinked a few times, then proceeded to call the next troop number.

We entered the dining hall a few moments later. I tried to laugh things off.

"That's the last time I go commando at camp," I said to the boys. A few of them laughed. The others just kind of sat there like they didn't know how they were supposed to feel.

I sat down with my patrol and we started eating. From my seat I could see Mr. Jackson surrounded by adult leaders and the camp director. He was gesturing with his hands and laughing, like he was trying to play the whole thing off as a bad joke. I winced and one of my patrol mates gave me a brotherly jab in the shoulder.

"You alright man?" he asked.

"Yeah. That was just fucking weird," I replied.

We finished eating and I lost track of where Mr. Jackson was. I tried to just put the whole thing out of my mind. As I exited the dining hall, Mr. Friday and a few other adults walked up to me. They'd been waiting.

"You alright, Zach?" Mr. Friday asked.

"Yeah. That was a bad joke," I replied. Mr. Friday and the others frowned, knowingly. Scouts aren't supposed to lie, and I think they could tell I was holding something back.

***

I didn't see Mr. Jackson the rest of the time at camp. When we got home from Parsons, Mom asked me specifically about him and what happened.

"One of the other adults called me and let me know," she said.

"Mr. Friday?" I asked.

"He told me," the Tyrant answered, emerging from the garage. It was a rare moment for him. He proceeded to make a big deal about something that was actually a big deal for once.

Shortly thereafter, Mr. Jackson ceased his involvement with the troop. And I tried to forget about it.

Later, I became an Eagle Scout. That award marks me for life. I feared my experiences would too.

19

Bus Ride

Location: Gig Harbor, WA (Southwest of Seattle) &
Maple Valley, WA
Age: 17

I met Kelly at a debate tournament. I'd seen her at team meetings but had never spoken to her. She was slender with black dyed hair and dark eyeliner.

We met when she watched one of my debates at Gig Harbor High School. I was debating the morality of the use of nuclear weapons. In debate rounds, you never know until a few minutes before whether you are arguing for or against a resolution. In this case, I was to argue against the use of nukes, which was my actual position anyways.

My opponent's case primarily rested on the need for America to win World War II, as our form of government and accompanying political values were morally superior to the alternatives that existed at the time. He argued that the use of nuclear weapons had precipitated the end of the war. During cross examination, I asked him if he knew when the Soviet Union entered the war against Japan. He was annoyed, "Well, they were our allies, so... probably at the beginning."

My case, which prevailed in the end, was that nuclear weapons had been entirely unnecessary, had been used specifically with post-war US-Soviet relations in mind, and that the Soviet entry against Japan was the decisive moment that led to Japanese surrender. After all, we had been destroying entire cities for a while at that point, and the Soviets declaring war on Japan was sandwiched in between our nuking of Hiroshima and Nagasaki.

Kelly seemed impressed by my routing of the nonchalant affirmative case. She had been writing in a notebook when he was talking, but as I proceeded with my case, I had her undivided attention. *She must agree with me about nukes.*

All debaters have their actual opinions on the resolutions. The hardest part of debating was when you had to argue against what you believed. It was a useful intellectual exercise though, as it taught you to reassess your own opinions after establishing a contradicting view.

As strange as it may sound, debate kids often find romance or sex over discussion of nuclear weapons, abortion, regime change, and other controversial topics. The thought that she may agree with me was why I initially approached her, on my way out of the room. After introducing ourselves, I got right to the point: "So, what do you think about nuclear weapons?" I asked with a smile.

We talked a bit about nukes, but I had another round to get to and had an oratory event later that day. For the oratory I was doing JFK's address in Berlin. I'd been practicing his accent. To my surprise, Cathy and Kelly showed up for the oration. Kelly seemed amused by my attempt at the Kennedy accent. The judges disagreed.

"You sound more like Mayor Quimby than Jack Kennedy," one remarked after.

"Oh, did you know Jack Kennedy? Was he a friend of yours?" I asked. The judge chuckled.

"How old do you think I am?" he asked.

"Pretty old," I replied, then walked away.

When I received my trophy at the end of the day, for debate and not oratory, I could see Kelly clapping and smiling in the crowd.

The team boarded the bus to head back home. It was going to be a long drive back to Maple Valley. As I walked down the aisle to grab a seat, my tie worn loose, and trophy in hand, I saw Kelly sitting alone. She was sitting close to the window, with plenty of space next to her. I paused at her seat, she looked up and smiled. I sat down.

There was a brief silence, but then I noticed she was playing with her hair, so I felt confident. There was the rumble of the bus engine starting and then we were off.

"How did you do at the tournament?" I asked.

"I didn't place, but my rounds went well."

"I'm happy about my oration despite what the judges said. I was so nervous about it but enjoyed it quite a bit."

"It was pretty cute actually," she said, playfully glancing up at me. And then we kissed. She gently put a hand on my face; I put one on the back of her head. I peeked and saw her eyes were closed, head tilted to the side. Then there was a tongue. Our tongues wrestled with each other. This went on for a few minutes, until Mr. Williams' voice rocked us out of it. He was speaking on the bus speaker system.

"Hey guys, we're uh… we're trying to have a professional ride home, okay?" he said, with a knowing look on his face. He was one of those cool teachers who knew how teenagers were and only stepped in when he had to. It was easy to talk to him about life without worrying about judgement.

I glanced around and saw that all our teammates had vacated the seats close to us. It must have been awkward when we started making out in front of them. Kelly blushed and pressed a hand to her face. Her other hand rested against mine. I took her hand in mine and smiled. She seemed like a nice girl and I liked that she appreciated my speeches. Most of the other girls in school ignored guys like me, at least that's what I thought.

Her chewing gum ended up in my mouth. There was a faint taste of cinnamon to it, must have been Big Red. I gripped it with my teeth and smiled at her. "Ha ha, I was wondering where that went." I peered over the seat in front of us and saw Mr. Williams had faced ahead again. I leaned in and kissed her, both hands on her face, and gave her the gum back.

I put an arm over her head and she leaned forward to let it down, to her shoulder, then leaned her head against my chest. *This is going well.* We sat like that for several minutes, as I pondered what to do next.

She's pretty. She seems smart. She likes my speeches. She's nice to me. I don't think she's dated anyone I know. I like kissing her. Why not keep this going? Maybe she'll be my first girlfriend. What will everyone think? She doesn't go to my church, so that won't fly. Making out with someone on a bus doesn't sound very Christian. Can I take her home to meet my family? How will she respond when he cuts me down in front of her? He always does that. What if she wants to do more than I'm comfortable with? If she doesn't go to church, does that mean we might have sex? Should I? What if I freak out again? Cathy hasn't really talked to me since then. She saw me crying on the way to the bathroom. I'm sure of it. What if I lose a debate round in front of her? What if I forget my lines during an oration? What if I don't get to be club president next year? Will she think less of me? Her hair smells nice.

I kissed her on the top of her head. "Your hair smells nice." She kissed my cheek. She put a hand on my thigh, with the pinky edging towards my junk. *Oh man.* I had a boner when we were making out—it was a halfy at this point—but I could feel it resurrecting. *Yeah, I think this girl would have sex with me eventually. That's awesome. I'm not supposed to though. What if no one knew? People heard about me getting a hand job from Cathy the night it happened. You can't keep secrets on a debate team. Everyone involved likes talking way too much.* She moved her hand to the inside of my thigh. A cold sweat formed on my forehead. *Dammit.*

In my panic to avoid another episode, I flipped the script. I moved my right arm down her back so that my hand was on her right hip. I slid the tips of my fingers into her pants. "Oh," she said.

I slid my hand all the way into her pants. She turned her body so her back was leaning against my chest and her right leg was bent, with the knee pressed against the side of the bus. She rested her head next to mine, then looked at me with worried eyebrows, as if she was wondering if I was going to be nice to her or not. I smiled and gave her a kiss, then moved my hand further down. She closed her eyes, smiled wide, and pressed her back against me. I started fingering her.

A few minutes later, she tilted her head back and pressed hard back against me, then she shook a little, and pulled my hand out of her pants. We were just pulling into Maple Valley and were only a few minutes from the high school, where my Ford Explorer was parked.

"Do you need a ride home?"

"No, my dad's picking me up at the school." We kissed a bit more and then pulled into the high school.

"Oh, shit there's my dad," she said as she pulled away. She waved out the window at him.

The bus parked and we all got up to leave.

Kelly disembarked the bus with no further show of affection, save for a smile and a wave when they were driving away. Mr. Williams frowned and shook his head at me as I got off the bus.

I encountered Colby on the walk to my Explorer. "What was that about?" I asked.

"What, the part where we all ran away from you guys, the part where you were SUPER unprofessional?" He teased.

"No, I mean, why did she just go distant like that when we were getting off the bus?"

"Her family is hella religious."

I got in the green Explorer, let it warm up, then headed home. The drive home was terrible. I had blue balls and a headache. I was beating myself up for freaking out again. I figured it was never going to work out for me with women.

***

The next day at school, one of my friends from church came up to me to inquire about the debate tournament. He wanted to know what happened on the bus. As I feared, word had spread. That wasn't even the worst of it. One of my frenemies on the team had been jealous or something and made a point to tell my mother about the whole thing when she was sitting in the stands at a swim meet.

"Zach, did you mess around on the bus with some girl?" she teased over dinner a few nights later.

The suspicion I drew from my church friends and questions from my family, made me uncertain about pursuing Kelly. I was still worried what would happen if we went any further than we already had. One girl already knew I was weird about having my junk touched. I didn't need a second one knowing. So, I ignored her completely for the rest of high school. I doubled down on church instead and signed up for my first mission trip to Mexico. I thought it would make me feel safe again.

20

I'm Done

Location: Maple Valley, WA
Age: 17

The Tyrant and I walked into the Safeway grocery store to pick up Chinese food for the family. It was a school night during my senior year of high school. I was anxious about college but had already been accepted to both schools I applied to and felt less concerned about grades as a result. My perfectionism was slipping, along with my tactical conformity, as I realized I was nearing freedom. Freedom from my status as a nerd. Freedom from having to go to church twice a week. Freedom from my family and this painful childhood.

We walked over to the little Chinese food section by the deli, not saying a word to each other. I was most enthusiastic to be away from him when I graduated, and it seemed like he knew it. He was no longer able to physically abuse me, as I was just over six feet tall now and lifted some weights. I was still chubby, but my arms were big. And during all the time that I spent growing, he spent it on the couch watching the news late at night, eating ice cream and sipping gin, until he became diabetic. He was in no shape to challenge me physically, and it was around this time that his gun collection started to grow again, along with his verbal attempts to cut me back down to size. I tolerated it, biding my time, hoping to escape unscathed and never see him again.

"Hello, what can I get for you?" the cashier asked from behind the till. I looked up at the menu.

"Sorry, I don't remember what I got last time. I need a moment."

"Sure, take your time." There was no one else in the line besides us.

"Oh come on," The Tyrant remarked from behind me. I ignored him, reading over the menu above. I needed to be careful because the last time we picked up food from here I got sick, but I couldn't remember if it was the orange chicken or General Tso.

"Hmmm. Hmmm. Hmmm. Hmmm." The Tyrant hummed behind me. I ignored him still. *I think it was the General Tso, because I asked who General Tso was and why chicken was named after him. Or was that the time before?*

"Can't even decide what to eat," The Tyrant remarked to a passerby. I peered over my shoulder. The other man sneered as he continued shopping.

"Hmmm. Hmmm. Hmmm. Hmmm." More humming. *The orange chicken looks good and I just feel like it must have been General Tso that made me sick. Let's go with that.* But before I could order, some young girls walked up with their mother. The girls wore soccer uniforms and were elementary school age.

"Look girls, he can't make up his mind," The Tyrant whispered to them. I'd had enough.

"WILL YOU CALM DOWN FOR ONCE IN YOUR LIFE?" I yelled at him, staring through him, like he had to everyone else. The Tyrant froze. A blank, dead look passed into his eyes. His face flushed. I turned back to the cashier.

"Yes, I'm sorry about that. Can I please get an order of orange chicken with some chow mein on the side?" I asked.

"Sure, no problem." The cashier plopped the food into a plastic container, put the lid on, and put it in a bag with some chop sticks and a fortune cookie. Then I paid and stepped aside. I raised my eyebrows as the Tyrant slowly walked up to the cashier. He wouldn't make eye contact with me, or with the cashier.

"Do you know what YOU want?" I asked him in the most condescending tone possible. He wouldn't look at me. His face was now bright red. He mumbled his order to the cashier.

"I'm sorry?" the cashier said. The Tyrant mumbled again.

"Oh, okay. No problem sir." More plopped food. The Tyrant pulled out his wallet and fidgeted with the dollars inside it. He placed them down in front of the cashier. The cashier pushed some of the money back at him, then took the proper amount and made change.

"Here you go. Thanks for coming. Have a good evening," the cashier said.

The Tyrant and I walked to his little, white pickup truck in the parking lot, not saying a word. I could always feel it when he looked at me. Now I didn't feel a thing. *Finally.* We drove home in complete silence. He didn't even try to turn on his damn country music.

When we got home, he dropped the family's food on the table and went to the garage. I put my food down on my placemat and sat. Mom was in the kitchen.

"Everything alright?" she asked. Mom was in jeans and a blue sweatshirt. She had a glass raised near her mouth.

"He was an asshole at the grocery store, so I told him to knock it off. I don't think he took it well."

"Oh, I see. What was he doing?"

"Just being himself. Trying to publicly embarrass me like he always does. He's been doing the same shit since I was a kid. It's not my fault he's such an insecure piece of shit."

"Zach…" she whispered.

"I don't care Mom. I don't care that he's a vet and his buddies got killed. I don't care that he's your husband. That was your bad decision not mine. I don't care at all. He's been an asshole my whole life. I'm leaving soon enough. That's exactly how I feel. Fuck him." I was like Kevin McAllister in *Home Alone. Do you hear me? I'm not afraid anymore.*

"This is going to be a great dinner," Mom said sarcastically.

"Yeah, just like every other dinner we've had up to this point. We're all going to sit there and wait for him to blow up over some shit. You're going to smile and redirect and cater to his feelings and try to put a good spin on things. Sarah and I are going to have to recite whatever B.S. comes out of his mouth. But I'm not going to do it anymore, Mom. All those nights, the only good part was your cooking, and we don't even have that tonight. I'm not going to give a fuck about his feelings. So, I hope you've got a plan."

Mom looked away, towards the stove. She knew I was finally beyond controlling. I felt bad for her. She was the one that had to sleep with him after all. I imagined that was just… awful. And I wasn't the only one who got abused in that house. But I told myself to not care. *You can't let her feelings stop you from standing up to him. He's wrong. He's been wrong the whole fucking time. It's not your fault he's addicted to pretending to be macho. It's not your fault he won't see a therapist and talk about his shit. "Stop crying like a girl." He thinks only women have feelings. Fuck him and his country music and his judgmental shit and all the hitting and spanking and yelling and public shaming.*

You don't have to take it anymore. You're going to college soon. You don't ever have to come back here.

The Tyrant walked back in the house. Mom hollered upstairs for Sarah to come down for dinner. Mom spread out all the food. We all sat down and started eating. I tried to use the chopsticks, which the Tyrant had always objected to, but I didn't care. *Maybe I think Asians are cool, asshole.*

Despite it not being Mom's cooking, the food was delicious. I was confident I'd chosen the right chicken. Sarah and I chowed down on chow mein and chicken. As I scarfed more and more, I noticed that Mom was eating slowly, and the Tyrant was hardly eating at all. I looked up at Mom. She was staring across the table at the Tyrant. I followed her eyes and was confronted with the most horrifying thing I had seen in my life up to that point. It was worse than the dead body I saw when I was four years old at that car accident. It was worse than Uncle Bobby's smirk. No, when I looked across the table, I saw malevolence like never before staring directly back at me.

The Tyrant's face was gaunt and saggy. It was a pale white now, with some sweat on the forehead. His jaw was completely relaxed, causing his lips and mustache to droop down to the laziest frown. And his eyes, staring right through me, were bloodshot with dilated pupils and angry eyebrows curled down over them. The dark circles under his eyes appeared more pronounced. I was alarmed that I hadn't noticed him watching me all this time, that I'd let my guard slip. *And where are his hands?* They were under the table. It occurred to me, that he kept guns in the garage. I swallowed hard.

"Honey… honey… everything alright?" Mom asked. The Tyrant smiled at me. His big, dumb smile. Powerful again. He carried that smile as he shifted his focus across the table to Mom.

"I'm going to kill your son," he said, cold, matter-of-fact. Things became fuzzy.

The next thing I remember, I'm running up the stairs to my bedroom. There are footsteps behind me, but their sound is lighter than mine. *Sarah.* I get to my room and close the door then collapse next to it. I hear Sarah's door close, too. "OH MY GOD," I heard through the wall. Sarah sounded hysterical.

There is yelling downstairs and then I hear the garage door open and close. That heavy door slams shut. *He's getting a gun.* My heart is pounding, and I can hardly breathe. My peripheral vision begins to narrow as I force myself back to my feet and make way to the window. I try to slide open the window, but its stuck. I pull harder and harder, crying now. *I don't want to die.*

I realize a moment later that the window is locked, and flip the lever to unlock it. I hear the garage door slam again and more yelling. Now Mom sounds hysterical. I slide the window open and step on my desk. I punch the screen out with my hand and climb out onto the sloped roof. Fortunately, there was no rain that day, so my footing is decent. I hear footsteps coming up the stairs. I butt-slide down the roof and drop myself to the hood of his white pickup truck; *crunch.* Then I run down the street, limping from how I landed. Things get fuzzy again because the running made it even harder to breathe.

The next thing I remember, I'm hiding next to a basketball hoop in a cul-de-sac in my neighborhood. I'm drenched with sweat and my hands are shaking. *Why was I dealt this hand?* Then I laughed a little and thought of C-3PO and R2-D2 on Tatooine. *We seem to be made to suffer. It's our lot in life. Me and the British robot and the loyal trash can.* I laughed some more. It must have sounded peculiar because a man opened the door to his house and tilted his head sideways at me. He must have been puzzled to see a boy from a different part of the neighborhood laughing loudly by himself next to a basketball hoop, with no ball or anyone to play with, alone in the darkness. I decided I had nowhere else to go but home.

I didn't hear police sirens or gun shots, just the cool, quiet of early night. I assumed that meant the crisis was over and that it was going to be swept under the rug, like most of the things that happen in the suburbs. *If no one has protected me so far, why would tonight be any different? My best bet is to just survive this and then never come back.*

The streetlamps were on now, over the sidewalks, and I heard an airliner flying overhead. One of my neighbors was working in his garage on a car. The door was open, and I could see him lying down tinkering. The rest of the houses were dark, save for the bluish glow of televisions coming through their living room windows. *Kevin Arnold was wrong about the suburbs. These houses aren't bound together by love. They're living in denial. Pain and struggle of love, my ass. No one's struggling for love. They're denying how they treat their children and themselves and they're covering it up with television and toys. Most of the time they don't even know what they're trying to do. It's a fucking charade.*

I walked up to my house; the baby blue paint and white trim seemed ominous now. The Stars and Stripes swayed gently on its pole, illuminated by a small light below. The same people were inside that house, or so I assumed, but things were different. They'd been made different several times before. I hoped this would be the last time.

I saw Mom sitting on the front porch steps, waiting for me. I stood on the sidewalk and looked at her. I'd been conflicted about her for a while. It was like she was almost powerless, but not quite, and what power she had, she was incompetent at using. I tried to tell myself it was because of her trauma. I tried to tell myself that it was because she was trapped, kind of like me. But I couldn't help and wonder, *What type of mother wouldn't call the police?*

"Zach?" She said from the steps.

"Hey Mom."

"Why don't you come inside?"

I laughed.

"Do you think that's a good idea, Mom?"

"He said he was just joking. He just wanted to scare you."

And you believe that?

"Okay. Is he going to apologize?"

"I don't think so. I think it's better we not talk about it."

"You're sure he's not going to do anything?"

"Yeah."

"Okay." I sighed, as I ascended to the front door and entered the place I was legally required to be for a few more months.

I took off my shoes, turned down a hug from Mom, walked up to my bedroom, and laid wide awake in bed the rest of the night. I heard Sarah crying in her bedroom and thought about going over to talk to her but was too exhausted. Too exhausted to speak or listen and too scared to sleep. *I'm alone.*

21

What Could Have Been

Location: Maple Valley, WA
Age: 18

I met Alexa on my first mission trip to Mexico. She lived a few towns over and went to a different church and school. But we stayed in touch with AOL Instant Messenger and grabbed lunch about once a month.

During my second trip to Mexico, I spent time with her again. We gave each other back massages while overheating during sermons.

I went to prom with a different girl, a girl who basically asked me, and I knew for sure Alexa liked me by the face she made when she found out. She went with one of my friends, and we didn't talk at all at the dance, but I caught her looking at me a few times. Longing eyes with pursed lips trying to deny how she felt. It was the only dance I ever went to in high school.

I took my weight more seriously towards the end of senior year. Jogging became part of my routine and eventually I worked up to five miles a day, five days a week. I lifted some weights too and had not been introduced to alcohol yet. I was looking and feeling better than I had in a while. The asthma had seemingly gone away.

The summer after graduation and before college, I started hanging out with Alexa frequently. We were both keeping up appearances at our churches at that point, slowly drifting away, knowing that we were both going to be sinners in college. We went out more often and I enjoyed talking with her. She was a bit girly at first, but anytime you wanted to talk about something serious, like politics, that act faded, and you found out how smart she really was. I got the impression she was still figuring herself out, trying to reconcile her brains with that body and how guys treated her and what she wanted from them and the world. She was sweet, and she was searching, and I always thought she wanted something serious though she would never admit it directly.

A natural chemistry emerged, and she was the only girl I ever brought home to meet Mom. Mom liked her, but was engaged elsewhere, putting out fires in her marriage and working at a daycare until school started back up. After the death threat, they made their third attempt at therapy, where the Tyrant behaved as usual, with walls up and no feelings discussed, assuming always that therapy was a conspiracy against him, that it was just some cudgel for others to assert authority with. I was glad I didn't have to attend like their previous attempts.

He increased his gun collection again, with the addition of a Vietnamese edition of the S.K.S., apparently rare, which he explained to me the "go*ks" used to shoot at him. Their sessions were on a regular schedule and kept them both out of the house at opportune times that summer. They were always gone Tuesday evenings until around 7:30. With their jobs also, that meant the house was left to Sarah and I for about 12 hours those days, and Sarah was usually at friends' houses instead.

I invited Alexa and a few friends from youth group over to the house on one of those Tuesdays. We played Risk, then went out back to the hot tub, one of the Tyrant's impulse buys. I'd asked Alexa if she wanted to take a dip before she came over, so she brought a swimsuit and I had one from inside but everyone else was in shirts and gym shorts. Alexa sat down in the bubbles right next to me and the others knew what was going on. We all made small talk for about ten minutes, then she kissed my cheek and rested her head against my shoulder and, one by one, everyone else quietly left.

We sat there for a moment enjoying the bubbles and heat. Then I kissed her forehead and she smiled. We kissed, and I told myself not to panic, that this one would be different. We made out for a while and I had my hand in her bikini bottom, then Mom opened the sliding door and said it was bad to be in the hot tub for so long and we got out. I guess I lost track of time. We dried off and made awkward smiles at each other, then she went home.

***

I saw her again a week later, but this time we went out for dinner and took a drive after. I was feeling good about this one. We weren't in love, but I could feel that it wasn't just a physical attraction. She cared about making a good impression with Mom and was sad for me when I explained why they were in therapy again. I thought maybe she would be my first girlfriend and we would do the long-distance thing in college, since we weren't going the same places.

I was driving her back to my place after dinner. The plan was to watch a movie. Her car was parked there. On the way back, I noticed the bus lane gate to Glacier Park was open. I contained my smile and turned in, driving down the lane as it curved along the school, then proceeded back to the basketball hoop next to the field. I parked my Explorer and turned it off.

"I have a big blanket in the back," I said.

She glanced out at the field, then looked down and smiled, playing coy. I leaned over and kissed her. She smiled some more. Then there was an intense, knowing look in her eyes and we both got out in a hurry. I grabbed the big blanket from the back, hoping it was clean. It was last in use at a soccer game a few months earlier but was dry and didn't smell funky. Besides, we just needed it for laying on.

We joined hands and went through the small opening in the chain link fence and out into the field. It was a clear summer night. The lights from the school were all turned off. The trees around the field were black and formed jagged outlines in the night sky.

We were almost to the middle of the field when it happened. A different type of panic, my eyes looking around at the trees, feeling like I was floating away to outer space, where I would suffocate and die. An urge to flee back to my Explorer, back inside where it was safe, overwhelmed me. Agoraphobia is what it was, though I didn't know that back then. All I knew was that I freaked out in open fields or along flat stretches of highway or other exposed locations, like the hill at Gas Works Park in Seattle.

I stopped to collect myself, trying to will my body to shut the fuck up. It had only happened a few times in the past year and never before then. Alexa turned back to me and kissed me, her body pressed against mine, what seemed like all my blood rushing downstairs. That brought me back. I didn't feel afraid anymore. *Maybe this will work out.*

I spread the blanket out and we laid down. The grass was dry, and the blanket was thick enough that it wouldn't matter if it wasn't. It was warm out, probably sixty-five degrees. We started to make out and eventually were both naked. I remember feeling entranced by her body, illuminated in the moonlight. I'd touched two vaginas before, including hers in the hot tub, but had never seen a naked woman in real life. A nice woman with a beautiful body on the ground waiting for me. I felt like Taj in *Van Wilder*. *You are the culmination of my being.* I was decidedly aroused.

A car drove by the field—I could see the headlights through the trees—out on the main road by the houses. I started to scan the trees in each direction, anxious again. Trying to coax me back to the moment, Alexa reached up and gently grabbed my cock, and that was the end of us. For a moment, I didn't know whose hand it was. I was looking at the trees when she gripped it and was filled with terror. I looked down and she was smiling and looking at it, rubbing it a little, but it was already going soft. I could feel it. My forehead tingled, letting me know that the sweat was starting. I let out a small cough as my chest fluttered, then knelt next to her, trying to breathe.

"Did I do something wrong?" She asked, blaming herself.

It didn't work out that night for us. Our second attempt a week later was no better. I blamed the whole thing on God. We were both still going to church anyways. "Jesus would want us to wait until we're married." She was disappointed but understood.

22

Am I Gay?

Location: Kent, WA
Age: 18

I got an idea stuck in my mind that maybe I was gay but just didn't know it. Maybe that was why I could never do things with girls without freaking out. I didn't know who to talk to and was overdue for my annual physical, so I scheduled a doctor's appointment.

I always feel uncomfortable when I get that first whiff of sterile cleanliness walking into a doctor's office. *The air smells clean but feels thick, and clean isn't supposed to be thick.* My disgust typically abates by the time I sit down in the waiting room, as long as I'm seeing my regular doctor and not a random one. My name was called, and I went with the nurse to an exam room for all the basic stuff, blood pressure, what are you here for today, weight and height.

"Oh, you've lost some weight. That's good," the thin lady said. Then, I sat and waited some more.

The doctor came in and we slipped into the regular routine. He checked my breathing and ears, had me move my legs around to check the knee joint, and had me open my mouth and go "Ah." I always brush my teeth before seeing the doctor, even if I've already brushed earlier in the day, because I don't like the idea of blowing foul air at someone trying to examine my throat for me.

I forgot why I had come until he got to the "turn your head and cough" part. He got down on one knee and I dropped my shorts. I didn't look. It felt awkward to. When he handled it, sweat formed on my forehead and I couldn't muster much breath for the coughing. Then I just let it out, while he was kneeling in front of me, one latex hand on my balls.

"Doc, how would I know if I'm gay?" I asked. I think that's the only time I ever made him feel uncomfortable.

"Uhhhh what?" he stood up, evacuating his hand.

"I'm just wondering. Can I be gay and not know it?"

"What are you talking about?" I felt embarrassed, my cock and balls out in the open and him flummoxed in front of me.

"So... every time I'm with a girl, I dunno, it just doesn't work out."

"Be specific, what happens?"

"I'll be with the girl and then when she tries to touch my dick, I kinda freak out."

"Are you aroused before then and then lose it?"

"Yeah."

"It could be a lot of things but considering your age, it's likely you're just really nervous."

"So I'm not gay?"

"Do you ever think sexually about other men? Either their bodies or them doing things to you or vice versa?"

"No."

"Do you masturbate?" I nodded. "Who do you think about when you masturbate?"

"Girls I know and some celebrities."

"Female celebrities?"

"Yes."

"Okay. I mean anything is possible, but in my opinion, this is just stage fright and not homosexuality."

Stage fright didn't make much sense to me. I'd thought it through beforehand with Alexa. I knew there was a chance I wouldn't last long my first time. I also knew she was a virgin too and would have nothing to compare me to. The thought of blowing it easily hadn't struck me as something to be afraid of. But he was the doctor, and I'd learned to listen to them. So, I assumed it was just nervousness from then on.

23

Indecision

Location: Maple Valley, WA
Age: 18

In late August, I ditched my plans to attend university. It seemed ironic yet inevitable that I did. For all my desire to leave Maple Valley, and especially to get away from my home, I grew increasingly tethered to the place as summer marched on. It was like I was a small child again, fearful of the world and unwilling to venture out into it, believing that things could only get worse. I felt unworthy of success and like I wouldn't find it even if I tried.

One of my friends went to college the year before. I visited him one weekend. He was a smart guy, but most of the people I met up there didn't seem particularly intelligent. I questioned if college was actually a place where people got smarter, or if it was just a rite of passage of some kind. We went to one party, where I didn't drink, but I watched others imbibe, their bodies coalescing in sloppy attraction for one another. Intimacy, which I desperately wanted but was becoming cynical about achieving, appeared to be the only benefit of going to college. The *Van Wilder*-esque way that everyone went about it though, drinking and getting laid, scared me now.

I told Mom I wasn't going to go to college and she nearly broke down in tears. After all she'd been through, she had looked forward to having a child go to college, to see one of her descendants gain positive yardage for her team. I felt bad about disappointing her.

The Tyrant and her had been in therapy for longer than ever before, which made me think he'd be around for a while. We wound up on speaking terms a few months after the death threat. I was uneasy about living with him, to say the least. I told him I was having doubts about going to college.

"Well, you could always start out at a junior college. Save some money and see if ya like it," he said that day out in the garage. The dusty garage with dim lighting and all his tools.

So, I enrolled at Green River Community College. A few friends and I commuted each day in my Ford Explorer. The classes were easy, and I held straight A's all quarter.

Most of my friends went away to college, either to Seattle or Ellensburg or Bellingham or Pullman. One decided to pull a fast one on us and run away to New Mexico of all places. I started getting drunk dials from my closest pals, pals that had been just as awkward and nerdy as I'd been, if not more so, regaling me, telling me how fucking awesome college was. I felt like I missed the boat.

One day, after I got back from classes at Green River, I hopped on AOL instant messenger and chatted with my friend Michael. Michael, or Mikey as I knew him, was a nerd like me, but he never appeared self-conscious about it. It was at his house that I watched my first porno. And it was he who talked me into going to college.

"mang this is fucking sweet," he typed on AIM. Mikey had watched *Scarface* a few times. We never typed properly online.

"Is it really that cool? are classes hard at all?"

"oh man no. no. classes are cake until you get into your major. thats like junior year stuff."

"done any drinking?"

"that's the best part zach. everyone drinks and everyone gets along and the girls are really nice."

"i feel like im missing out. green river might have been a mistake."

"you could always transfer up here for winter quarter. got a few more days until the deadline to apply."

"oh shit. yeah, im gonna do that. thanks man."

"be good to have ya up here mang."

And that was it. That was when I decided that college was for me. I even knew where I wanted to go: Western Washington University. It was where Mikey went, and they'd already accepted me once before.

I sloppily applied in a state of exuberance and wrote an admissions essay about self-doubt that might have been too honest. They let me in.

24

Clean Slate

Location: Bellingham, WA (Northwest WA, along Pacific Coast, close to Canada)

Age: 19

Mom dropped me off at my dorm early on a Saturday and was emotional as moms often are in such situations. Then she left, off to fulfill her New Year's Resolution to divorce the Tyrant without telling me. I had to hear about it a few months later when Sarah accidentally spilled the beans via text. Why Mom kept me in the dark is a mystery to me, though I would guess it was guilt. I had already lived through one of her divorces.

The dorm was Edens North and I was on the first floor in room #144 with a yet-to-arrive roommate. Shortly after Mom left, I was unpacking in the room and heard a knock at the door. I opened it and there was Mikey, my friend from back home. Mikey had always struggled with his weight, as had I, but he had slimmed down a bit in college, especially around the face.

"Sup mang!" he greeted me.

"Dude, what are you doing here? You live on this floor?"

"Yeah, I'm in room 136, just four doors down. I got a half rack. Wanna help me polish it off?"

I didn't know what he meant by half rack or the thing about polish, but I was bored with unpacking and happy to see a familiar face, so I followed him a few steps down the hall and into his room. Mikey opened his minifridge and inside was the first beer I would ever taste: Olympia. We cracked them open and clinked them together. "Cheers mang. Welcome to college!" he said.

After struggling through my first can, Mikey pulled out a beer bong and, wisely, led me down the hall to the community bathroom for my first go at it.

"We'll just do one can for you and just remember, lean over here," he pointed at the shower, "if you need to puke."

I didn't care if I puked at that point, but I didn't. I paused halfway through the bong to let down a big gulp and then Mikey raised the bong higher in the air and I let the rest pass. I was Thanksgiving full and then let out a loud, long belch and no longer felt that way. The belch brought up a small amount of beer foam and I gulped it back down.

Mikey was a hygienic drinker for the most part and rinsed out the beer bong after each turn. He got down five and I did three. We were in the community shower for about an hour, just two 19-year-old men drinking and laughing amongst ourselves. Then we headed back down to Mikey's room for more beer.

At that point, walking down the hall back to his room, I knew I was drunk and felt so happy about it, like I was free and had gone through a rite of passage of some kind. I stumbled once then started sliding my shoulder against a wall. The beer in his room now tasted like carbonated water and we chugged the last of it down.

Then Mikey got out the bottle that I was to have a love hate relationship with for the next year: Bacardi 151. It was a fresh bottle; he had just been re-supplied by a 21-year-old on the women's floor above us. He pulled out a knife.

"See you gotta cut through this flame suppressor shit otherwise it pours funny," he explained matter-of-factly. Mikey was always full of useful information.

He took out two shot glasses from his computer desk and poured them each full. He handed one to me and I made the mistake of taking a whiff of it.

"Oh man... that will definitely make me puke. I'm sorry dude."

"No worries mang, you just need a chaser. Grab some Coke in the fridge."

I grabbed a can and opened it.

"Now, just take half the shot and then sip some Coke right after. Then do it again."

We gently clinked glasses and then I did as instructed. Drunk or not, it burned like hell and I almost did puke. Even with the Coke there was a spot of fire in my stomach for a few minutes after.

"Feel bad to waste the rest of the Coke," Mikey said as he handed me the bottle. "This is a good trick for fooling the *Resident Advisors*. Just pour some Bacardi in the can and they won't know the difference."

"Shit, I didn't even think about them," I replied.

"They come by around 8 PM on weekdays and again at 11 PM for quiet hour. Weekends are 2 AM. They come back if they hear noise or get a complaint. Closest one is one floor above us. Cute brunette. Kinda short."

"Ever been caught?"

"Yeah, they make you take a $50 class about how if your dad is an alcoholic that makes you one too," Mikey imitated masturbation as he said it.

"Shit but didn't your mom get mad?"

"Shows up as a miscellaneous student services charge. They make you take the class, but they don't narc on you."

"I'm kinda surprised by that," I said.

"It's good for the university if you really think about it. This isn't Yale or something. If our parents found out we were all getting shitfaced out here, they'd hesitate to pay."

"Yeah, that makes sense," I laughed.

I sat down in a chair at Mikey's roommate's desk. He hadn't arrived yet either. "Where is everyone anyways?"

"Most people are coming back tomorrow or the day after. It isn't like fall quarter where there's a rush to move in."

I took a sip of the can of Coke and Bacardi. It didn't taste like Coke anymore, but I kind of liked it. I sat the can down next to the bottle on the desk and stared at it for a moment while Mikey fussed with his computer to put on some tunes. I felt relaxed. Like I could take on the world. I felt warm inside and like I didn't care about Mom or the Tyrant or the girls from high school or how difficult everything had been up to this point. *I've got a clean slate.*

"So, how are the girls here?" I pointed up at the ceiling.

Mikey smiled.

25

Beer-pong

Location: Bellingham, WA
Age: 19

I quickly settled into a routine in college. Classes were a cakewalk freshmen year. I had no idea how easy school could be when you only went three hours a day and there was no busy work. The exercise regimen I began towards the end of high school was quickly added to my college routine, albeit at a rec center that made my old gym look like crap. I had a meal plan, so there was no cooking, and I had no job. All my classes and studying and working out was accomplished in about 5 hours a day, leaving the rest for drinking and meeting new people.

No one cares that you're a nerd in college. I was also pleased to find out that basically everyone I met had no knowledge of my hometown or anyone in it. No one knew how shy or awkward I had been. That knowledge, coupled with a better physique, alcohol and, eventually weed, gave me the confidence to approach women that I would have considered out of my league before.

My success rate surprised me. I'm not talking about sleeping with someone. I'm just talking about the responses I got from women when I flirted with them. That's all I considered success at first. Then came the drunk make outs. They would always go one of two ways. Either one of us would leave during the night when the making out was over, or one of us would leave in the morning before the other one woke up. We never had sex and we never talked about it, but the same women would reliably come back the next time I was drinking in the dorms. Maybe they thought I was a nice guy because I'd kiss them and hold them and sleep with them but wouldn't grope them in the night or try to fuck them when they were slurring. Or maybe we were all just trying to figure ourselves out. I don't know.

Eventually I went to my first off-campus party. It was there that I found out that some women will kiss me before even knowing my name and that women can forget names too. *Have I always been this attractive? Or are we all just being casual about this?*

It was at one of these off-campus parties, after a few rounds of beer-pong with a female partner I just met, that I got the feeling I might get laid. After we lost our third round, she grabbed my hand and took me to a makeshift dance floor in the kitchen.

I was double-fisting beer from our defeat and basically just stood there while she grinded on me. This went on for a few songs, with my hands moving to her hips as I finished my beverages. Then she leaned her head back and yelled so I could hear her over the music.

"Do you smoke?"

"Only pot." I had never smoked cigarettes because I thought they smelled like my father's apartment. And I preferred to not think about Papa, though I made sure to call him every week. Why, I'm not sure. Maybe it's because I knew no one else would.

"Let's go," she took my hand and smiled as we walked out on the back deck. It was quieter out there, though the bass made the sliding glass door shake.

When we got there, she turned to me expectantly. "Oh, I don't have any." She smirked and gave me a playful punch in the chest.

"So, which dorm do you live in?" She asked.

"Edens North. What about you?"

"Fairhaven. You like it?"

"Yeah, the R.A.'s haven't caught us yet, which is nice."

"I should come by some time."

"Yeah you should."

Her voice sounded like Tara Reid, who I had a crush on back then, after watching *American Pie* a dozen times and *Van Wilder* 32 times. But she didn't look like Tara Reid. She was a brunette and vaguely Mediterranean, maybe Italian.

"Do you know anyone who lives here?" I asked.

"Yeah, Mark is in one of my classes, but he's visiting his parents this weekend."

"So, he's not here?" I leaned in.

"No, he's not," she gripped my shirt with her hands. We went back inside and walked down the hallway from the kitchen, then up the stairs to Mark's room. After we closed the door, I realized I didn't know her name.

"Ummm… my name is Zach."

"Ha ha, Stephanie."

We got close and started kissing. I reached over and turned the lock on the door. Then we took our clothes off and moved to Mark's bed. *Don't freak out.* I was hard as a rock and really wanted this to happen but had a nagging feeling it wouldn't. She reached up and put her hands on my face and kissed me some more as I climbed on top of her.

151

"Are you okay with this?" I asked, looking in her eyes.

"Yeah," she replied, her eyes looking down me as I got in position.

Then I entered her. And I was very surprised by it. Instinct took over. The bed slammed against the wall over and over. She started making those oddly exciting female noises where you think she's really enjoying it, but it also sounds like she might be dying. This confused me, so I slowed down and stopped.

"Why are you stopping?" She asked. She thrusted her hips down, inserting me into her again. *Okay then.* I resumed slamming the bed against the wall.

Afterwards, I laid down next to her and she turned to cuddle, and I held her for a while.

"Can I get your number?" I asked.

"Yeah," she smiled.

"You gonna come by next time we party in Edens?"

"Oh yeah," she smiled and kissed me.

I got her number. We cuddled and kissed for a few more minutes. Then, I checked the time.

"Shit, my ride is probably leaving soon. It's almost two. Do you need a ride?"

"No that's okay."

We kissed again, then got dressed and walked downstairs together. I scanned the room and realized my ride had left me behind.

"Shit, he's not here."

"Let's walk back."

So, we walked a few blocks back to campus along N. Garden Street, then up to Edens North. About halfway, she jumped on my back and I gave her a piggyback ride the rest of the way.

"I guess I'm your ride?"

"Yes." She kissed me on the cheek.

26

Morning After

Location: Bellingham, WA
Age: 19

I woke up in the morning surprised to find a woman in my arms, head resting on my chest. It all came back to me and I smiled more than I ever had before. A tear rolled down my cheek. *I finally did it.* I slid out from under Stephanie and made my way to the community shower, toothbrush and paste in hand.

Stephanie walked in when I was halfway through brushing. I spat in the sink.

"Excuse me, miss? This is a men's room."

"Mmhmmm. Got any mouthwash?"

"Yeah, some Listerine in the closet on the left in the room." I resumed brushing.

Stephanie came back a few seconds later, swishing her mouth and making that look of pain that someone with a dirty mouth makes while using Listerine. She frowned and made some faux pouting noises while the liquid burned her tongue. I spat and rinsed my mouth with water from the faucet.

"Only dirty girls get burned by mouthwash," I informed her. She turned her head sideways at me, eyes wide, but still swishing. Then she spit it out too.

"Oh really?" She pressed up against me. I was looking in her eyes when a covert hand cupped my balls. I tensed up. She grabbed my face with her other hand and kissed me. She tasted like Listerine and old memories. Memories of Cathy and the hotel room. Lips locked, I peered out with one eye at the mirror and thought of the time I cried. I felt her slowly rubbing me. My heart fluttered, and I reached down with both hands and picked her up, removing her hand from my crotch in one motion. She looked down at me and brushed some moisture from my forehead, then kissed me again.

I walked her back to Fairhaven, across Western's endless walkways of bricks, with a few jutting up, causing me to stumble. We made plans to meet up that weekend. She wanted Wednesday, which was 420, but I'd already made plans with the guys on my floor to get really stoned all day. I could have invited her to that, but I needed some time to process what had just happened. I didn't understand how I'd had sex, how I was able to. It didn't make logical sense to me. *Was it just the alcohol? Was my doctor right about it just being stage fright?*

27

Hot Box

Location: Bellingham, WA
Age: 19

I woke up to the sound of shouting out in the hallway. "MERRY CHRISTMAS! MERRY CHRISTMAS!" I rolled over and squinted at the clock. It was 12:00 AM on the dot, on 4/20. Doors flung open from the other rooms. I jumped from my lofted bed and opened mine as well.

"MERRY CHRISTMAS! MERRY CHRISTMAS!" It was Gary, our resident thespian. He was skateboarding up and down the hall, shouting, waking everyone up.

"Shit, Gary!"

"COME ONE, COME ALL!" Gary waved for everyone to follow him down the hall to his room.

A disheveled Mikey sauntered to the hallway, wearing a bathrobe and shorts. He tilted his head back and laughed a loud "YES!" when he realized what the commotion was.

About 12 of us staggered into Gary's room, clad in pajama pants and gym shorts. The rest went back to sleep, having early morning classes. A few women from the floor above came down too. Some brought their own supplies. Others acquired pipes and papers from the desk drawer that had been generously opened for us. Gary's room would have been the R.A. room if one lived on our floor. He had his own bathroom as a result. We crammed ourselves into that little bathroom of his, a few sitting on the rim of the bath tub, some sitting on the sink, one on the toilet with a woman on his lap, and the rest standing shoulder-to-shoulder, stacked against each other like sleepy sardines.

Mikey walked in after making music selections on Gary's computer. His jam back then was "Blueberry Yum Yum" by Ludacris, which had just come out the year before. He put it on, a few heads in the bathroom nodded in approval, and everything started getting passed around. Not much talking, just the sound of lighters being sparked, the bubbly noise of a bong, coughing and giggling, and Ludacris singing to us all. All snug together in Gary's little bathroom, until it got hazy and hard to see.

I took a hit off a small pipe that was passed to me. I'd only smoked three times before and was still very much a newbie. I adjusted my seating on the bathtub and then took a hit off a joint that got passed my way. It hurt, and I coughed and nearly dropped it, but Mikey reached over and took it from me before I could.

"Our buddy here is still new," Mikey said with the joint between his lips. He took a powerful hit, then stopped and took a baby pull, then sucked it all in deep, puffing up his chest, holding it for a moment, then letting it all out and passing the joint along.

My coughing subsided just in time for a bong to show up in front of me. "Shit man, I dunno about this." I confessed.

"Just take a little one," Gary said.

"I've never used one before though."

Gary and Mikey crouched in towards me and showed me how to pull the bowl out to clear it after I had some smoke. Gary lit a corner of the bowl and I inhaled slowly. Water percolated as the tube filled with smoke. "That's probably enough," Mikey said. I pulled the bowl out and inhaled as fast as I could. I started coughing aggressively. Then there was a hand holding my hand, retrieving the bowl from it, and another pulling the bong away from me, so I couldn't drop it.

"Holy fuck," I managed in between coughs. Gary cleared the last of the bong.

"Zach's getting a lot of new experiences this week," someone laughed.

"Lost his virginity at that house party on Garden," someone said. I couldn't tell in the haze.

"Nice man. Sounds like those lungs just lost their virginity too." A bit of laughter, then more lighters being sparked and the sound of inhaling.

I was still coughing. The room was foggy and one of the women from the floor above opened the door and stepped out. I got up and followed her, making sure to close the door quickly behind me. Gary's room was easier to breathe in. I coughed a bit more, then got back to normal. There was an appeal to going back into the bathroom for more, but I was already feeling the effects and didn't want to overdo it. I meandered down the hall and back to my room.

Lying in bed, I felt happy and like everything was hilarious. My legs had been sore from jogging but were now rubbery and at peace. I rubbed my face against my pillow and it was heavenly, like I could stay there forever. I reached over to try and set an alarm on the digital clock but knocked it to the floor instead. I rolled around in bed laughing about it. I started to think about Stephanie and how I could have sex now somehow. I reached for my phone and thought about calling her. One unread text message showed up as I flipped it open. It was from her.

"Heeeeeeey. Hows 420 in edens? Im in mathes with some friends."

What luck. Mathes was on my side of campus, not a long slog away like Fairhaven. I started to feel horny. I clicked reply and started typing.

"ITs crazy over here I am so high right meow haha"

A moment passed and then came her reply.

"So what you doing now?"

"Just laying in bed. I think I broke my cock"

Nothing for a few minutes. I looked at the message again. *FUCK!*

"CLOCK I meant clock. Wanna come to edens? ;-)"

"Yes :-)"

I spent a few minutes convincing myself to get out of bed. It was so comfortable, but I needed to open the door to the building, so she could get in. I sat up and hung one leg over the bed, then there was a knock at the door.

"It's open!"

The door opened, and Stephanie walked in.

"Shit, how did you get in?"

"Someone was walking in when I got to the door," she replied.

"Come here," I said.

She smiled and climbed the ladder to my lofted bed. She laid on me and we kissed. Her hair was damp and smelled nice and familiar.

"Did you just shower?"

"Yeah."

"Do... do you use Pantene Pro V?"

"Ha ha. You are such a dork. How do you know that?"

"I... I smell it at Hairmasters. It's the shampoo they use on me when I get my hair cut." I lied. They used Paul Mitchell with Tea

Tree Oil. I know how it smells because I used to use it myself but was insecure about admitting that.

"Mmhmmmm. Is your roommate here tonight?"

"Yeah, he's down the hall smoking still." My roommate was a cool guy. He was into weightlifting and *Counter-Strike*.

Stephanie kissed me and gave me a look, then glanced at the door. I slid off the bed, stumbling as my feet hit the floor. I chuckled. I grabbed a sock from my drawer, opened the door and tied it to the doorknob, then closed the door and locked it. I moved my mouse to wake up the computer and searched for a song to play on my Windows Media Player. There were footsteps coming down the hall from Gary's room. They approached my door.

"Oh shit, what the fuck is this!?" They were standing at the door now.

"Oh, shit man! Get some!"

Feeling funny, I selected "When A Man Loves A Woman" by Percy Sledge, and turned the volume up. Upon hearing the first lyrics, laughter erupted in the hallway.

"You are SUCH a dork," Stephanie joked, laying up in the bed.

I crawled up the ladder and back into bed with her. There was still conversation in the hallway.

"Don't you feel weird with your friends right there?"

"Hey baby. I didn't brag about it. They know we got together cuz they were at the party too. All I told them is that I like you a lot. They're happy for me and they're stoned. Don't worry about it. My roommate doesn't even have class tomorrow."

"You really like me huh?"

"Yeah."

"How much?" She looked in my eyes, then looked down herself, then back up at me, asking me to do something to her without asking out loud.

"I'd like to do that for you, but don't judge me cuz I've actually never done that before."

159

She smiled, and I went down on her while Percy Sledge sang to us.

"Oh my god. This is your first time?" Stephanie asked in disbelief. Her head tilted back, one of her hands on her chest and the other on her forehead. She repositioned her hips and one of her legs slid out wider. I felt encouraged, like maybe I was a natural. I kept going, my own arousal growing with each of those little sounds she made. Percy was done and "Come As You Are" by Nirvana started playing.

Towards the end of that song, Stephanie arched her back and her legs straightened out and there was a hand grabbing at my hair. "Please don't stop." Another hand grabbed my head, holding me tight. My face was trapped. If my nose had been stuffed up, I probably would have suffocated down there. What a way that would have been to die.

"Don't stop. Don't..." And then there was silence, her whole body went rigid. I kept going and then she exhaled loudly, and her body relaxed, and she slowly pushed my face away from her. Her legs closed as I backed away, and I stared at her.

"A dork AND A LIAR," she teased, as I crawled back up next to her. I don't think I was a pro at it at first, but it didn't seem nearly as complicated as *American Pie* made it out to be, like you needed a secret book to understand how to do it. Maybe she was one of those lucky women who orgasm easily. Or maybe I just hit the mark with her.

We spooned for a few minutes, listening to Eminem now, then I poked her in the ass. She moaned and turned her head and kissed me. I put my hand on her hip and pulled to turn her over. She complied. I moved on top of her and spread her legs again. Then the song changed and Christina Aguilera's "Genie in a Bottle" started playing. I was embarrassed.

"Christina Aguilera huh?" She laughed at me.

I held her face in my hand and kissed her then looked in her eyes.

"Yeah?"

"Yes."

I entered her for the second time. I don't know how long I lasted. The clock was on the floor and my trigger was harder to pull while stoned, especially that stoned.

Lying there afterwards, with Stephanie in my arms on that little twin bed, I told myself it was over, that I'd made it past my previous difficulties. Life was finally looking up.

28

Another Party

Location: Bellingham, WA
Age: 19

I didn't see her for about ten days after that. We both had midterms coming up and were going through the motions of caring about our grades. Once that was done it would be smooth sailing until finals, giving us a couple of weeks together until saying goodbye for summer. She was going home to Oregon and I had a job lined up in Maple Valley.

An upperclassmen business major at the University of Washington had messaged me on Facebook, asking if I wanted to paint houses. It was the only offer I had so I took it. I knew I was going to party a bunch over summer, but figured I'd save some cash, stay in shape, and get a tan if I worked outside. As long as it wasn't landscaping.

After midterms were done, I got stoned and drunk with some of the fellas. We did it in Gary's room again. There were more women this time. A pretty blonde from Higginson, which was just across from Edens, was there and we chatted for a while. She leaned up against me and it made me feel guilty. I made like I was going down to Mikey's to grab more refreshments but really, I wanted to get away from temptation. Stephanie and I weren't a real couple per the standards of our generation—it wasn't on Facebook—but we had agreed to not see anyone else. She was on the pill and we both agreed condoms didn't feel nice, though I'd never used one. She still didn't know she was my first.

I got down to Mikey's room and he was sipping a forty of Mickey's Ice.

"How's the party?" Mikey asked.

"It's cool. More women this time."

"Yeah, one of 'em hates me from fall quarter. Girl came in and sat on my lap and said nice things to me, then got cold and distant a week later." I figured there was more to the story but didn't press it.

"Got another one of those?"

"Yeah, help yourself mang." I reached in the fridge and grabbed a forty. Mikey and I had an unspoken system where I would drink his alcohol and would then chip in cash on the next liquor run to make up for it. We liked drinking the same things, so it worked out.

We drank a bit and reminisced about growing up together. Then we smoked a little pot and Mikey passed out on his bed. I walked out of the room and heard music playing down the hall but thought better of it and went to my room.

I put on an episode of *Southpark*, which I'd downloaded illegally, and sat on my bean bag sipping some Bacardi 151 and Cherry Coke. "Quest for Ratings" came out the year before and I liked it even more since I started smoking pot. When it got to the part where Butters gets naked and runs through the street, I got an idea and was drunk and stoned enough to try it out. I checked the clock: 3:00 AM. I texted Stephanie, grabbed my keys and changed into gym shorts and a T-shirt, then walked outside.

I strolled from Edens across Old Main and to Red Square. I went past it up towards Artzen Hall. There was no one around, just me and shadowy maroon buildings and bricks that tried to trip me. I jogged back to Red Square, stripped down, and jumped into the fountain. I splashed and swam around, then relaxed and floated on my back. Cold water feels good when you're hammered.

The experience made me reflect on my childhood. I went streaking nearly every week when I was a teenager and I felt the same excitement somewhere deep in my mind now. Some part of me that was frantic and raw, which I didn't understand but felt compelled to embrace. Sometimes I didn't even remember leaving my house, my mind snapping back to reality as I frolicked under lamp posts, mist gathered around their light. The color, a dull yellow, always reminded me of Papa's apartment.

A few minutes passed, then I opened my eyes and saw Stephanie sitting on the ledge, illuminated by the glow of Red Square's lamp posts. Her hair was messy and she was in pajamas with a blue Adidas jacket on. I stood up and walked over to her.

"Cold out huh?" She smiled and looked down my body.

I moved my hand back as if to splash. Stephanie hopped from the ledge and backed away.

"Don't fucking do that." She laughed.

"Cold out huh?" I mimicked, "DO WOMEN NOT KNOW ABOUT SHRINKAGE!?"

She brought a towel like I asked. I dried off and got dressed. We went back to my place, drank some more Bacardi, and had sex until morning.

29

Dead Week

Location: Bellingham, WA
Age: 19

I was feeling very confident about college and my life by the time dead week arrived. I was having regular sex, partying, still had good grades, and had a job lined up for summer. What more could I ask for at that point? Stephanie and I agreed that we needed to tone down our social lives to focus on finals. Our last exams were both on a Wednesday and move-out wasn't until Saturday, so we made plans to party hard the last few days in the dorms and then say our goodbyes.

The problems began for us one night studying together in Wilson Library. It was late, well past midnight, the library having extended hours for dead week, and we had found an empty study room. I was reading through my notes from Environmental Science 101 about the Kyoto Protocol and she was working on her final paper for English. We'd been studying together for days and had been very productive, but there was a tension in the air. We hadn't done it in about a week.

"Have you heard about those students who got caught having sex in the library last quarter?" She asked, looking up from her notes.

"No, I haven't. What happened?"

"Well, they were down in the old little room that no one goes in. One of the custodians walked by and saw them."

"That sucks." I flipped to my next page of notes.

"It was just poor timing on their part. Everyone knows most of the staff is gone by 10."

"Oh, I see. Why're you telling me this?" I smiled.

"Just making conversation." She made eyes at me, then looked down at her notes.

"Mhmmmm." I opened my textbook, scanning the highlights I made earlier in the quarter.

"You know, I was thinking earlier about you licking my pussy and it made me really wet."

"So, where is this small room?" I chuckled.

We got up and left our study room. The study rooms were well-lit and had glass walls. There were other students out there studying who could easily see us. We left our belongings behind and Stephanie led me to that small room. It was unlit and a bit dusty, like it was never used. There was a typewriter sitting on one of the desks.

She leaned against a desk and I kissed her. I reached in her sweatpants and started fingering her. She shoved her tongue in my mouth, then her hand wandered from my chest, down to my stomach, and then further down. She could feel my erection pressed against her leg. Her hand slipped in my gym shorts, searching for it. *Don't fucking freak out.* I was having one of those boners that goes down the pant leg instead of up through the waistband. She reached down my boxers and found the end, then clutched the thing. "That's the cock I want," she said, pulling her face away, looking in my eyes. But I was somewhere else.

"Babe, what's wrong?" I had stopped fingering her, my hand motionless in her sweatpants.

"Nothing's wrong." She started to rub it, but to no avail. It was deflating fast.

"You sure baby?" She kissed me on the cheek. I wiped my free hand against my forehead. My old friend the butterfly was dancing around in my chest.

"I'm just worried about getting caught. Come on, let's get back to studying." I pulled her hand out of my shorts.

"Wait, what?"

"Come on."

"Hold on, when have you ever been worried about getting caught? Your friends in the hallway or skinny dipping in the fountain…"

"I just want to make sure I do well on finals, that's all."

"Okay," she said with disappointment in her voice.

We got back to studying but I could hardly focus. *Dammit. I've already had sex with this woman a ton. Why the fuck is this happening now? It is just the booze and weed isn't it?* Stephanie got up to go to the bathroom. I grabbed my things and bolted.

I started crying on the way back to the Edens North. "What the fuck is wrong with me?" I said aloud. My pocket buzzed. A new text from Stephanie.

"Are you okay? Where did you go?"

"I'm not feeling well. Gonna go to bed."

"…ok."

30

Farewell

Location: Bellingham, WA
Age: 19

I didn't see Stephanie the rest of dead week. We texted a bit but studied separately. We made plans to meet up once finals were done.

My last exam was finished at noon on Wednesday and I was wiped after, having not had any sleep for the past few nights. I went back to Edens and took a nap for about an hour. Stephanie's last exam was done at 3:00 P.M. After the nap, I sat in my room feeling nervous. I walked the hallway and no one else was around. I got out the bottle of Bacardi 151, about a third of the fifth left, and grabbed a can of Coke from Mikey's room. I'd never drunk alone before, but I didn't know what else to do. I poured myself a drink, a stiff one.

I pounded that one, then poured the rest of the booze into the can of Coke and walked out for Fairhaven, texting Stephanie. I reached Fairhaven and walked in with a crowd through the locked doors.

"How were your finals?" She asked as she opened the door to her room. Her roommate's bed was bare. She'd already moved out.

"Good, I think. I'm just glad it's over with."

"We need to talk." She had a serious look on her face.

I took a sip out of the can. "Okay. What's up?"

"That's not just Coca-Cola is it?"

"No."

"Zach… I don't know how to say this. Like, we're not serious but we've only been seeing each other…"

"Just come out with it. Don't take your time."

"It's occurred to me that we only have sex when you're drunk or stoned."

"Or both."

"Yeah… or both." She looked down, then after a moment back up at me, eyes full of concern. "Why is that? I thought the time in the library was very unlike you until I realized it's the only time we've tried something sober. And you freaked out and ran away."

"I didn't run away."

"You left without saying goodbye the moment I left the room."

"Okay."

"So, what's going on?"

"I don't get why you're upset."

"I'm not upset." She stepped towards me; palms open at her sides.

"But we're having this serious conversation now when we're supposed to be celebrating. My exam was done before yours. I got a head start."

"Can you not fuck sober?"

"I don't know." I shook my head and turned away.

169

"What do you mean you don't know?" She touched my hand.

"You're the only one I've been with." I made eye contact, but only for a moment.

"I find that hard to believe. No other opportunities?"

"Well, yeah. I had some opportunities before college. They didn't pan out."

"And why is that?"

"What do you want from me?"

"I just want to know if you can't do it sober and why that is. I know we're not like in a relationship, but we've been spending a lot of time together and I'm just worried that you might have issues. One of my friends got assaulted and she said that it affects how she has sex."

"I have issues? You go upstairs and fuck a guy on someone else's bed, the night you meet him. I bet if I hadn't asked your name you wouldn't have known mine before we did it."

"So, I'm a slut or something?"

"That's not what I said. We started all this at a party. Is it really that crazy to think that I like to party, and I like to fuck, and I like you? Since when is that an issue?"

"Well... but you still freaked out. And, I kinda felt like you freaked out a little that first morning, in the bathroom. You just suddenly grabbed me and picked me up like you didn't want me touching your cock."

"I don't know what you're talking about."

"Okay. We're not doing it unless you're sober though." She
Was frustrated.

"What?"

"If you won't tell me what's going on, this is how it has to be." *Just like the counselor and teachers in school.* And I hated her for it, too.

"Goodbye." I walked out the door.

"Zach!" She followed me to her doorway and watched me walk down the hall. I never saw her again.

31

Homecoming

Location: Maple Valley, WA
Age: 19

When Mom and I got back home to Maple Valley, I stood in the driveway for a few moments, unable to move forward. The baby blue paint and white trim house appeared the same as before, except the flagpole. It was still there but no longer had a flag flying. I imagined a sad bugle playing as the Tyrant lowered the Stars and Stripes between gulps of a gin and tonic, before beating a hasty retreat that became a guerilla campaign. Yes, Mom had divorced him. Yes, he was stalking Mom now. She found his cigarette butts outside, by the windows, piles of them. One night, she swore she saw him through the kitchen window. Another night, when she was suspicious and scared, she went outside—which I lectured her about later—and found his truck with matching license plate a few yards down the street but couldn't locate him.

Terrified, she bought a gun. It was the first one she'd owned since Papa's pregnancy gift all those years ago.

That wasn't all that had changed at the house though. As I clomped up the small wooden steps of the front porch, I glanced back at the grassy front yard and noticed someone had been ravaging it. There was a small, yellowed section closest to the steps, and clumps of dug up dirt and grass littered everywhere. Mom was always conscientious about her plants, spending hours out in the yard gardening, watering when the sun was down. I was confused how this could come to pass. *Was she so preoccupied with not being abducted or killed that she'd neglected her hobbies?*

I carried my bags in through the front door and kicked off my shoes. There was a flurry of small feet. It sounded like it was coming from the den. The flurry got closer and then a beast leapt up to the dining room. It became a scratching, flicking noise, as it sped towards us along the hardwood floors. Then, it barked at me.

"Woah! What the hell is this?" I exclaimed, dropping my bags, preparing to defend myself. I'd play-wrestled with black labs and basset hounds as a child but had never encountered a German Shepherd before. It is a breed simultaneously elegant and endearing, yet vicious and menacing. And this one, a bit on the fat side and clearly older, was also damaged goods.

"No no," Mom reassured the beast in the same voice she used on me when I was a child. "It's okay." The beast cozied up to her leg, a bit unaware of its own size and strength, causing Mom to lose balance and take a step back. His eyes were locked on me. He was black and light brown, with wisps of white around his eyes and mouth, and a thick tail.

"So, a gun and a German Shepherd huh?" I commented.

"He's a rescue. Poor guy has had a hard life," she said, her gaze alternating between me and the dog, who she petted now. It made me want to cry for some reason. I looked down.

"What's his name?" I asked.

173

"He doesn't have one yet. Maybe you have an idea?"

"I think I would if he'd stop looking at me like I'm lunch."

"Come here," Mom said to me. I stepped forward. The beast attempted to lunge, but Mom grabbed his collar and reassured him. "It's okay. It's okay."

I extended my left hand, because I'm right-handed and consider the other hand expendable, holding it in front of the beast's nose. The space just above his eyes twitched, as he pondered my hand, then eyes up at Mom, then at my hand, and then her again. He sniffed, then licked his nose, and his tongue ran along my fingers as he did. I leaned forward and petted him.

"Good boy," I said.

"See?" Mom asked.

"Yeah. We'll see when you're not around." But I knew it wouldn't be anything to worry about. His tail started to wag as I pet him. His mouth opened, as if to smile not bite, and I saw his teeth were misshapen and some were missing. He was a broken, scared dog, not a mean one. "What's this here?" I asked as I pointed at his open mouth.

"Oh, they didn't know at the shelter. They think his previous owners filed his teeth down, or that he was locked in a cage for too long and lost teeth gnawing on the wires trying to get out," Mom said. She made a sad smile.

The beast stared at me now, like his dark eyes were peering into my soul, like he already knew exactly who I was. I abandoned my bags and walked upstairs to my room.

I named him Thor. I thought it was a manly name for a dog.

***

That summer I spent my days hungover on a ladder, painting houses and swatting away wasps, and the nights drinking and smoking cigars with the boys. Our meetup was a gazebo on the golf course up the street from my house. We fancied ourselves cigar connoisseurs, but all we could afford was grape Swisher Sweets.

Mom planned the family trip to Ocean Shores for the Fourth of July, but I told her I couldn't go because of work. It was a lie. The boys and I had a party at the house while she was gone, raiding the remnants of the Tyrant's liquor cabinet, plus a bottle of Benedictine and Brandy, which I believed to be left over from Papa.

That party was the closest I got to a woman all summer, but the encounter only left me hating myself more. We made out on the futon in the den. I could tell that she liked me and might want to do more than just kiss. She asked which bedroom mine was. And I balked at that, telling her in a drunken haze that I was the host of this party and had to make sure all my guests got home safely. She disappeared from the party about an hour later with another woman, leaving the rest of us a sausagefest.

That night I felt like a fool, like a dumb, scared little fool. I didn't want to count how many times I'd run away from good opportunities, but I counted them anyways while slurping from Papa's old bottle. It wasn't so much the prospect of ejaculation. I'd had that plenty. Rather, it was intimacy. I'd known this woman for a while. I knew she was thoughtful and trustworthy and sweet. I knew she could have made me happy. And even if we hadn't been good together, I knew for certain that at least one of the women up to this point would have been a good match. *Why does this keep happening to me? Why can't I figure this out?*

Dark thoughts crept into my mind. I tried to shun them with more booze, but they were insistent. I began to have a dreadful feeling that this is how it was always going to be. That even though women are good, and even though some of them want me, that none of them were going to slow down their lives while I figured myself out, if I ever did. And none of them were going to dive into the deep end to save me from drowning. All these women, anyone of whom could have been a good partner for me, were going to carry on, with normal men, starting families, buying homes, leaving me behind. I felt like I did the day my parents divorced, like I was scared and hiding in a cold bathroom, alone in the world, even though I was surrounded by friends. I tried not to cry. I was the host after all.

Things became blurry as I blacked out. The evening became a swirl of brief sequences in the backyard, my friends laughing and yelling together. Eventually the liquor ran out.

The night reached a crescendo as two friends vomited on the back deck. I helped them back inside, to the bathroom, then went outside to turn on the hose. I was startled to find the vomit was gone. A fat, old dog sat on his haunches where the vomit had been, licking around his mouth.

"OH GOD!" I yelled as I bent over, trying to suppress my own urge to puke. I looked back up and winced like I'd just observed a friend in an embarrassing predicament and didn't want to make things worse by judging. But I couldn't help it. "Bad dog!" I whispered aggressively at Thor. He stopped licking and tilted his head to the side at me. I made a mental note to give him more kibble from then on.

***

Mom protested the amount of food I gave to Thor. She was the one that put him on a diet in the first place. So, Thor and I jogged together as a compromise. Jogging with that old, fat dog, is the only healthy thing I did that summer.

And before long a few of my friends went back to school, as they were on the semester system, and then, one by one, my remaining friends departed too. I stood alone in my bedroom and said "I'm not coming back here again," but I had the sneaking suspicion that I was lying to myself once more. I packed up and headed back to Bellingham.

.

32

Sophomore Year

Location: Bellingham, WA
Age: 19

Buchanan Towers was a different living situation than Edens North. There were four people per unit, with two bedrooms divided by a common living area and kitchen, and one bathroom with a shower. Being compartmentalized gave it less of a community feel than Edens, as everyone could just stay in their unit, never venturing out for cooking or pissing. The first thing I noticed walking down the hall to my new home was that no one left their doors open. I was going to live with my friend Kevin, a shorter guy who didn't drink and loved playing basketball.

Kevin and I got situated, he took the top bunk in our room, and then our suitemates arrived. Blake and Travis were both freshmen. Blake liked baseball and drank. Travis was lanky with bleached hair. He smoked tons of pot. Seemed like a good fit for me.

The guys from Edens North all lived off-campus now, but I had a buddy from Higginson who now lived on the top floor of Buchanan. Craig and I drank a bunch freshmen year. Buchanan was eight stories and Craig chose the top floor for its vaulted ceilings. After getting unpacked I went up to visit him.

"How was summer?" Craig asked while handing me a Miller High Life.

"Good man. Saved some cash. Found a cushy job after ditching painting. How about you?"

"Not bad."

"Miller High Life huh?"

"The Champagne of Beers," Craig quoted. We proceeded to get drunk.

Craig was an easy guy to get drunk with. His agenda was always simple. There were never elaborate schemes to go to this person's house or sneak into that bar or Facebook events to RSVP to. You just sat down and got drunk and saw where the night went. Freshmen year, that usually involved wandering around campus with non-alcoholic looking containers full of alcohol or socializing with whoever happened to be around on my floor or his. There was something else at play tonight though.

"So, Zach… meet the girls next door yet?"

"No, why you ask?" I asked, walking to the fridge for another beer. *The Champagne of Beers. What an odd thing to put on a can.*

"Well, there's this one girl living next to you. If you get a chance to invite her up here, you should. She's kinda punk. Petite, with red hair." Craig shrugged his approval.

"Okay, I will."

We kept drinking. Twelve beers down we got out a laser pointer and started shining it into other people's windows at their computer screens and walls. We didn't get anyone in the eye but annoyed the hell out of a dude trying to jack off to porn.

"Dude's so small I can't even see it from here. Ha ha."

"Know what the best part of living on the top floor is?" Craig smiled, then jumped up on the ledge of a window, whipped out his dick and pissed.

"Fuck yeah man." I jumped up on a ledge next to him, stumbled and fell back, then tried again after drunkenly convincing myself to be steady. I whipped mine out and pissed out the window, the urine spreading out a bit as it traveled eight stories down. Towards the end of it, I noticed a woman about ten yards from where our piss was landing, standing under the dim light of the building, waiting for us to finish, likely disturbed.

"Ha ha man, there's a woman down there."

"Shit, where's the laser?" Craig hopped off and went to his desk. He returned to the windows and started shining it down at her.

"REALLY?!" came a yell from the dimly lit woman. Craig and I retreated from the windows, laughing uncontrollably.

I stumbled down the hall to the elevator, took it down to my floor, got off and stumbled down my hall, but stopped at the door next to my suite. I was curious about this girl that had piqued Craig's interest. I knocked but no one answered so I went to bed.

33

The Girl Next Door

Location: Bellingham, WA
Age: 19

The next day I woke up with a slight hangover and went down the hall to grab Gatorade from the vending machine. On the way back, the neighbor's door was open, so I knocked gently.

"Hey," she said as she walked to the door. She had red hair, a pretty face, wearing red plaid pants with belts crisscrossing between the legs. *This must be the girl.*

"Hey. I live next door. Saw the door opened and wanted to introduce myself. I'm Zach."

"Stacy," we shook hands.

"So where ya from?"

"Boise. Just transferred this year to Western. I went to Boise State before." While she was talking, I noticed she had a tongue ring.

"Cool. Just wanted to say hey. Kinda hungover so I think I'm gonna take a nap."

Stacy laughed and played with her hair a little.

"You drink?" I asked.

"Yeah."

"Well, if you want. We're drinking again tonight. I don't have classes tomorrow ya know?"

"That sounds good." She gave me her number and smiled at me, then looked down like she was nervous. Despite the attire, she seemed more girly than punk. I went back to my room and slept a few more hours.

34

Irish-exit

Location: Bellingham, WA
Age: 19

The ringing of my phone woke me up. Groggy, I reached for it and squinted to see the name. Craig. I answered.

"What's up man?"

"Nothing. Wanna come up?"

"Yeah, just gotta shower then I'll be up. We need to make a run?"

"Nah, already got resupplied." Craig and I had a similar arrangement as I had with Mikey, though I eventually lost track and probably still owe Craig some money.

"Cool man. Hey I met that girl next door. I think the one you mentioned. I'll ask her to come up too."

"Sweet. I... I better shower too then." Craig laughed a little.

We hung up and I sent Stacy a text. "Hey. It's your neighbor Zach. Going upstairs in a few to drink. Wanna join?"

The response was nearly instant. "Cool. Yeah just knock when you're going up." I hopped out of bed and headed for the shower.

I got cleaned up and drank two large glasses of water, then dressed and brushed my teeth. Then I walked next door and knocked. Stacy answered and smiled.

"Good to go?"

"Yeah," she said still smiling.

We rode the elevator up. Craig greeted us with Miller High Lifes. I sat down on the couch in their living area. Stacy sat next to me. Craig reluctantly took a chair. We pounded the first beer and opened another, then another. Stacy was the first woman who ever kept up with us.

"So, you can drink huh?" Craig asked.

"Yeah, but too much beer will make me full."

"Got any hard A, Craig?" I asked.

Craig got up from the chair and opened the freezer. Ice cold vodka. The label was in a foreign language. Craig was part-Russian, so I assumed the vodka was Russian. He poured three shots and set them on the table in the middle of the room. We downed those and a few more, and a few more beers. Eventually things got slurry and blurry. Craig started explaining how he liked the lofted ceilings on the top floor because it meant there was so much more storage space. He didn't have too much stuff, but I guess it mattered. He went into his bedroom while talking and got distracted by something on his computer monitor.

"Hey," Stacy leaned over on the couch and whispered to me.

"What?" I whispered back. She raised her eyebrows and gestured to the door. *Oh... whaaaat?* I smiled. We got up and quickly left. It was the only time I ever Irish-exited on Craig.

We scampered down the hallway to the elevator, got in, and then watched the doors close. I turned to her and grabbed her. She put her hands on my chest and we kissed. The doors opened, and we walked down the hallway together.

"My place?" I asked.

"Yeah. My roommate has an early class."

We walked in to my room. Kevin was on his computer but hopped up and took a blanket to the living room without being asked. *Good guy.* Stacy and I started kissing as he closed the door. I started trying to trap her tongue ring with my teeth. She giggled and pulled away.

"Got a thing for tongue rings?"

"I don't know. I'm curious about them."

We kissed some more and made our way to the bottom bunk, my bed. I climbed on top of her. We made out for a while and I thought about pressing my luck. Craig liked the girl, but she hardly knew him, and I was liking the idea of beating him to her. My phone buzzed. I pulled it out. Craig. I chuckled.

I reached down to unzip her pants. Her hand met mine. I looked in her eyes. She blinked with raised eyebrows.

"What's wrong?"

"I'm on my period. I'm sorry."

"You don't have to apologize. That's fine. We don't have to do anything." I kissed her some more, then laid down next to her. She cuddled up to me and laid her head on my chest. Her hair smelled like strawberries.

"So why are you curious about tongue rings?" She stuck out her tongue.

"Well... you're the first woman I've kissed who has one and... I heard they make blowjobs awesome."

"My mouth is a bit dry for that," she teased. I jumped out of bed and walked funny to the kitchen, poured a large glass of water, and walked funny back to the bedroom. Kevin was watching *The Boondocks* on the TV I brought up.

"Ha ha." She took a few gulps. I laid down next to her. She kissed me then moved down.

Her mouth was a little cold at first, from the water, but that went away fast. I realized I didn't have a preference for how she did it, as I'd never had one before, so I just tried to relax and let her go with it. She seemed to have a good understanding of what to do.

35

Ice Cream

Location: Bellingham, WA
Age: 19

Stacy was lying awake when I woke up. She smiled, her head resting on my shoulder. "Good morning," she said.

I smiled. "Hey." I got out of bed and went to the shower. Kevin was passed out in an odd position on the couch. It looked like he fell asleep sitting up then leaned to one side. He woke up when I walked out.

"Thanks man, very cool of you."

"No problem," he said while stretching and untwisting his back. He had a pained look on his face.

I brushed my teeth and took a long shower. Stacy was gone by the time I got back to my room. I texted Craig.

"Sorry about last night man. Stacy wanted to head out."

"It's cool. We're at breakfast right now. Want to hang out later?"

"We?"

"Stacy and I went to breakfast. Her roommate Becky might be down to hang out later too ;-)"

Oh what the fuck is this? Does he not know?

"Sounds good man. Text me when you get started."

I walked next door and knocked. A blonde woman with a Cindy Crawford beauty mark answered. I stared for a moment. She smiled and raised her eyebrows at me.

"Hey. I live next door and wanted to introduce myself. I'm Zach."

"Becky. I'm Stacy's roommate. She said you might come by."

What the fuck is going on?

"Yeah. Hey. Do you drink?"

"Sometimes..." she smiled.

"Okay. Well, later we're all gonna have some drinks upstairs if you want to join."

"Sounds fun. Just text me when you're going." She gave me her number and I walked away confused.

I watched *The Boondocks* and grabbed lunch, smuggled some ice back from the dining hall in a Tupperware container, then started drinking. I figured I needed to get a little buzzed to deal with whatever I was going to encounter upstairs later. There was a bottle of Bacardi 151 in my desk, which I mixed with Coca-Cola. I downed a stiff one, then poured another and tried to pace myself.

If Craig still wants Stacy after what we did, then that's fine. Besides, her roommate Becky is pretty.

I texted Craig. "Hey man. Already got started. You down to hang?"

"You drinking? Who with? Becky?"

"Nah man. Kevin and I had one," I lied. Kevin never drank with me. I think he secretly saw my partying for what it was: a front.

"Sure, come on up. Stacy is here."

I texted Becky. "Hey, it's Zach. Heading upstairs to drink if you still want to join." There was no answer, so I walked next door and knocked. Becky answered, phone in hand.

"I was just texting you back. Let's go."

When we got up to Craig's room I was surprised by what I saw. Stacy was sitting in Craig's lap on the chair he reluctantly took the night before. I sat on the couch. Becky sat unusually close to me. I decided to just let things unfold.

There were empty cans on the table. Stacy and Craig had started in early also, perhaps for the same reason I had. We went three rounds of Miller High Life. Becky was struggling to keep up. She was so tiny; her body probably couldn't hold that much liquid.

"Craig, got any more of that vodka?"

"Yeah, in the freezer," he gestured with his arm in that general direction. He couldn't get up because Stacy was still sitting on him.

I got up and went to the freezer, retrieving the vodka and some ice cream I found there. I grabbed some spoons from the drawer, but there were only two. I poured a round of shots and we all downed it, then I handed a spoon to Craig. He took it and scooped some cookies & cream out, then turned to Stacy, and fed her.

"Do you want some ice cream?" I asked Becky and held up my spoon. She smiled and nodded. I proceeded to feed her. This went on for a while. Craig and I got a bite or two ourselves, but for the most part we were just spooning sweetness into their mouths. We had a few more drinks and Becky rested her head on my shoulder.

I went to take a piss in Craig's bathroom and when I returned, Becky was sitting in the living room all alone, and Craig's bedroom door was shut. *Oh, that's hilarious.* I looked to Becky. "Wanna get out of here?" She nodded and got up.

She kept close to me as we walked down the hall and into the elevator. While riding down I put my arm over her shoulder, she leaned in, then I kissed her. She kissed back, but her height made the whole thing difficult. I picked her up and we kissed some more.

Kevin was asleep on the top bunk, or at least he was pretending to be. Becky crawled into my bed and I set an alarm for 9:00 A.M. I had class at 10:00 A.M. We made out some more. I loved how soft her hair felt in my hands. The combo of sugar and alcohol and not sleeping much the night before did me in though, and I fell asleep.

Becky stirring in bed woke me up. I was aroused and had it pressed against her leg. She slid away from me. I opened the eye closest to the pillow to see what she was doing without appearing awake. She leaned over and kissed me on the cheek, then left. When the door closed, I checked the clock: 3:00 A.M.

36

Shattered Glass

Location: Bellingham, WA
Age 19

I got up hungover and made my now routine trip to the vending machine for Gatorade. I didn't care that Becky and I hadn't had sex, though I really wanted to, but my body had failed me and gone to sleep. The glow of the vending machine annoyed my eyes as I put quarters into it. I needed what was inside if I was ever going to make it to class.

Her name was Jenna and I met her by that vending machine. She lived a floor or two above and had just broken up with her Navy boyfriend. Dirty blonde, cute nose, athletic. She was fetching Gatorade also, though her attire and perkiness said it was for post-gym purposes rather than post-drinking.

"Hey!" came a chirp from behind me. I turned.

"Hello," I grunted.

"You live in BT too?"

Well obviously.

"Yeah, just down the hall actually."

"Oh cool. I'm Jenna."

"Zach," I opened my Gatorade and took a drink. It was like ice cold water after a long hike. "Just getting back from the gym?"

"Yeah, my boyfriend and I broke up a few days ago. He's in the navy and it just didn't work. Trying to sweat it out of my system." She let out a self-conscious laugh.

"That's too bad, his loss though," I smiled.

"What about you?"

"Oh... Well I'm hungover." I let out a self-conscious laugh.

"Doing some partying?"

"I do some. Yeah. Sometimes. You?"

"I would really like to." She made a familiar face. It's that complicated face where you can tell they're rebounding and would have sex with you but also might regret you later because they're so vulnerable now. I'd seen it tons of times on girls that I was friends with, the attractive girls who told me their problems and went on walks with me in high school, but I never made a move on them. My experience had taught me that guys who hook up with rebounding girls are somewhat unethical, since girls in that state are often looking for friendship and emotional support, not dick, but will sometimes trade sex for the support they need. It's a reluctant trade that my female friends told me they didn't really want to do, more that they thought it was the only way. Didn't seem fair, so I mentally friend-zoned those girls while pretending they'd friend-zoned me. *She's not a girl though. She's a woman. And this is college. What's the harm in just hanging out?*

"Wanna watch a movie?" I asked.

"Totally," she smiled. I decided East Asian Politics could wait.

We walked down the hall and she kept close to me like Becky had just seven hours earlier. *Three girls going to my room with me in three days. Nice.* I felt like the manliest man who ever manned. The feeling didn't last though.

I opened the door to my bedroom, to drop off my keys and phone, and was pleased to see Kevin was not there. I turned to walk out to the living room but didn't make it. Jenna had followed me into my bedroom. I had been right about the face she made. We weren't going to be watching a movie on the couch or on my bed, or anywhere for that matter. She closed the door. We were both sober, and I knew then that I'd made a huge mistake.

She pressed up against me and we kissed. She tasted like lemon-lime, or maybe I was just tasting myself. I thought about the Bacardi 151 in my drawer. *Maybe I can convince her to take a few shots with me first. It's morning. She'll never go for that.* Maybe it was the hangover, but the cold sweat started before we got very far. She gave me a gentle shove towards the bed and my heart fluttered. I sat down, and she leaned over to kiss me. I joined her but lacked enthusiasm and she could tell. She let out an uncomfortable laugh.

"What's up?"

"I don't know. I just feel really tired."

"Oh come on. Guys have harder boners when hungover. Just lay down." I let out a nervous giggle.

I laid down and she climbed on top of me and took off her shirt. Grasping her ass, I tried to talk myself past the panic that I knew was coming. *She's not trying to hurt you. When she touches your dick, just relax.* It didn't work. Grinding her hips as she kissed me, she could tell I wasn't getting into it. She smiled and moved her hand down my shirt towards my shorts. My hand met hers there and we stopped.

"What's wrong?"

"Nothing. I just don't know you that well is all."

"Just relax." She brushed some sweat off my forehead.

"I'M NOT FUCKING COMFORTABLE WITH THIS," I blurted out. Startled she got off the bed.

"What the fuck man?"

"What?"

"Look, it's cool if you're not down, but why did you bring me back here then? Feeling confused?"

"What the fuck is that supposed to mean?"

"We're at Western. It's okay if you're gay. Just don't waste my time." She put her shirt on.

"Get the fuck out of here."

"Whatever dude." She left.

That fucking bitch. I started drinking.

***

A week or so later, in a haze, I got a text message from a friend telling me that Craig and Stacy were in a relationship now. I swung to punch the wall but missed and shattered my bedroom window, spilling glass to the walkway below. Kevin was distraught.

37

Alcohol and Drug Consultation and Assessment Services (ADCAS)

Location: Bellingham, WA
Age: 19

The alcohol class was about how Mikey had described. What a jerk off that was. A serious sounding but clearly bored admin gave me the results of my questionnaire as if she was telling me I had cancer, but I was like the thirtieth person she'd given the news to that day. A lot of my relatives drink. My dad drinks a lot. That means blah blah blah. She sounded like Charlie Brown's teacher. Then we were taught about how to pour shots, since college kids are too stupid to measure things properly, or so it was implied. Some information on how to spot alcohol poisoning was passed around. A sad story was told about a student who died, not at our college but somewhere else.

I trudged back to my dorm, along Western's brick pathways, my pant legs getting wet from the puddles. I would have avoided them but had too much on my mind. Missing some classes and being told you're an alchy after damaging school property wasn't a good way to start sophomore year. Panicking in the bedroom wasn't either. *I thought I was past this.*

Bethany was one of those sincere helper types who seemed to worry a little about everyone. She was my R.A. in Buchanan and left a note at my door to come see her when I got back. She had short hair and was chipper. I'd only talked to her once before.

"You wanted to see me?" I walked in to her room, the door had been open.

"Zach. How are you doing?" She smiled as she leaned my way. *Oh man. She says it like she's signing me up for Vacation Bible School, but I don't see any Bibles.*

"I'm sure you know basically how I'm doing. I just got back from that class."

"Yeah. Look. I can tell you're not doing well and I want to help. Can you tell me what was going on when you broke the window?"

"I got some shocking news about a woman who sucked my dick once."

"...Okay." Her eyes were wide and she looked away.

"I'd been drinking because things didn't work out with a woman," I continued.

"The one who..."

"No, a different one. There were three actually. It didn't really work out with any of them, or the one over the summer, and I don't really like how I left it with a different one end of spring quarter last year. We were kinda a couple but also kinda fuck buddies but then she threw some serious stuff at me at the end and I left." I was oversharing because I was tired and didn't want to go through any more official processes that day. I knew if I sat down and confessed to her all my shit that she'd take notes like a wannabe therapist and refer me to the resident director who would probably freak out and want me to go see someone and I really wanted to sleep and just forget it.

"So... why do you think you drink?"

"To pass the time? Or cuz I'm in college and it's fun."

"Do you think it's possible that you're drinking to cover up something?" *Why are women always so clever about this sort of thing?*

"It's possible. But the class told me that it's probably because my parents drink a lot. Well, my mom drinks some, and my dad drinks a lot, and my stepdad drinks a lot, but I'm not related to him so that would just be an environmental influence, not a genetic one. Plus, mom already secretly divorced him."

"I see. Are you feeling okay?"

"I'm just really tired. I know I fucked up and I'm going to stop drinking for a little while, so I can focus on classes."

"Okay. I just want you to know that even though we don't know each other that well, I'm here for you. I think, personally, that your alcoholism is covering something up. I think you're in pain. I wish you'd talk about it, but I don't want you to feel forced." I was feeling oddly attracted to her. I kind of wanted to stay in her room and talk more and maybe ask for her number. *What are you doing? She's your R.A. and thinks you're trouble. She's not going to date you.*

"I appreciate that, Bethany. I'll stop by if I need to." I backed towards the door.

"Okay. Anytime. My phone number is on the placard next to my door." She smiled. *Is this woman trying to fuck me?*

I walked down the hall back to my room and was overcome with tears for a second, so I walked faster and then jumped in my bed.

38

Midnight

Location: Bellingham, WA
Age: 19

I woke up around midnight to a crashing noise.

"Oh my God. Again?" Kevin said from the top bunk.

"It's not me, man." I got out of bed. The noise had come from the living room. I opened the door.

It was dark, but I could see my suitemate, Travis, the bleached stoner, standing by his door, and a large black object on the floor between us. It took me a second, but I eventually realized it was my TV.

"Dude…"

"Dude, I'm sorry. I just tripped and knocked it over."

"Okay. Does it work anymore?" Travis turned a light on and we moved the TV back to the table it had been sitting on. I plugged it in and pushed the power button. Nothing happened. I looked at Travis.

"Dude, I'm sorry. I'll make it up to you. My bad man." He reeked of weed and his eyes were red.

"Okay." I went back to bed.

39

The Tyrant

Location: Bellingham, WA
& White Rock, British Columbia
Age: 19

I toned down my drinking for a month and focused on class. My first upper division courses were proving to be heavy on the reading. Very heavy. Who knew there was so much to read about East Asian politics? Between class and the gym and studying, I kept occupied. I completely ignored Stacy and Becky and I hadn't even seen Jenna since that encounter. No drinking with Craig. No drinking at all. It was like when I was a kid, with that drive for perfect grades at all costs. I lost some of my beer weight and went into midterms cautiously optimistic.

Mikey got ahold of me in early November. He'd moved off-campus to a condo his parents bought. "It's much nicer having all this space to myself. What you doing before Thanksgiving? Midterms are done for me the Friday before." Mine were stacked over the course of three weeks, starting the first week of November. We made plans to meet up after and celebrate.

"Dude you got your passport up here?"

"Nah, it's back home. Why?"

"My hookups aren't down anymore. Was thinking we'd go to White Rock to celebrate." Western was about 20 minutes from White Rock, B.C., where the drinking age was only 19.

"I'll ask my mom to mail mine up to me." And she did.

Having midterms stacked over several weeks was preferable to having them all the same week. It gave you time to focus on each one and recharge for the next. The only drawback is that you don't get a clean break from them immediately after. By the time the last one is done, you will probably already know how you did on the first, which I foresaw as potentially demoralizing. The situation doesn't allow for you to take your exams, forget about them for a week, celebrate some, and then find out later how you did on all of them. No, you had to go off to celebrate being done with midterms already knowing how you did, which, depending on the outcome, could be a huge buzzkill. To make matters worse, the first exam was on East Asian politics, my hardest class. I'd probably know that grade right before leaving for Canada with Mikey, though I guess alcohol helps with any outcome.

***

I crammed for a week before that first midterm. I hadn't missed any classes since I cut off the sauce either. My notes were pristine. The night before, I drank a Monster energy drink and re-read entire chapters of the textbook, committing all the parts I previously highlighted to memory. It turns out I'm sensitive to caffeine, along with everything else. This is how I found that out. Once I was done studying, I brushed my teeth and went to bed, and I laid there wide awake for a while. I squinted at the clock, begging it to tell me it hadn't been that long since I laid down, but it had been. It was 3:00 A.M. and class was at eight. *I'm fucked.*

I waited a bit longer, tossing and turning, but soon gave up and went to the stairs. I jogged up and down the eight flights of stairs for about 20 minutes, working up a good sweat. Then I took a hot shower and laid back down to sleep. I passed out around four, I think.

***

The alarm clock must have fallen off the window ledge when I got in bed that night. Or maybe I hit it with my arm while half asleep. Either way, it didn't wake me up. Kevin did. He hopped out of bed and went to the shower. The door opening got me up. I searched for the clock, found it on the floor, and nearly died when I saw it: 8:03 A.M. Class had already started. I put on shoes without socks, grabbed my keys and a pen, and ran to class in my pajama pants and a gray T-shirt.

It took about five minutes for me to run there. The professor, a short woman with short hair, sniggered and shook her head as I crashed through the door. I took a seat and started the exam, flustered and out of breath. *Am I dreaming? Is this a nightmare about my fear of not doing well on the test?* I pinched myself, hard. *Nope, this is real. I am so fucked.* I started to read the questions.

I actually got all the questions done in the time allotted, but I didn't feel very good about it. I walked towards my dorm feeling like shit and thought about drinking. Instead I stopped at the Fairhaven Commons to eat my feelings. Five bowls of cereal later, I went back home and slept most of the day.

The other midterms were easier. I felt good about them and avoided energy drinks when studying. One of the professors even told me my grade a few days after the test. An 'A'. I felt good about myself again.

***

November 22nd, 2005 rolled around. Mikey and I had agreed that was the day we were going to Canada. He was to drive, and I was to buy a few drinks for him when we got there. I wasn't quite sure how he'd sober up before driving back, and we had no hotel plans, but I didn't care. It was the anniversary of J.F.K. getting shot, which I knew because I fixate on stuff like that. That was also the day I got my grade back for the East Asian politics midterm. I'd been talking myself into a good mindset about it. *It's not the end of the world to not get an A. It is a hard class and the prof has a reputation for being hard. You're not the only one. If you get a A- or a B, that's fine.* She handed them back at the end of class. I got a C+. *FUCK MY LIFE.*

I wandered back to my dorm in a haze. I don't really remember the walk back. I was thinking about my stepdad for some reason. Or rather, my former stepdad. *I wonder what he'd think about this.* Back when I was a kid, bad grades on a test would mean grounding or worse. But if I got straight A's and came home to celebrate, he'd meet me with "Why do you think you're so smart? You're not that smart. You're still a little boy." Maybe he'd be happy I had failed. Maybe that's what he always wanted. It gave him a reason to be mean.

When I walked into Buchanan, Craig and Stacy were kissing in the doorway to her suite. Craig looked over at me mid kiss and waved with one hand. I couldn't tell if he was teasing me or just saying hello. I gave a half assed wave back. *Does he still not know? Are they throwing it in my face to fuck with me? I shouldn't let these fuckers get to me.*

Travis was washing a dish when I walked into the suite. He still hadn't paid to replace the TV he broke. "Dude, when are you gonna replace the TV?"

"I was thinking. Can I just give you a dub for it?"

"A dub sack? Like twenty bucks of weed?"

"Yeah, would that be cool?"

"What the fuck dude? The TV is not worth twenty bucks."
Lowballing stoner. Fuck him.

I went to my room and texted Mikey to see if he was ready. He was. I got dressed and put on some deodorant then grabbed my passport and walked outside to wait for him. He rolled up in his black, two-door Civic, and we were off.

We hopped on I-5 and headed north. Mikey had some electronic music playing, who knows who made it. He was feeling chatty and I wasn't, and he could tell.

"What's up mang?"

"Nothing man. Just kinda fed up right now. Nothing you did."

"What happened?"

"Got a shitty grade on one of my midterms. My roommate still won't replace the TV he broke. He tried to low ball me with a small sack of weed. And Craig and Stacy are flaunting their affection for each other in front of me. Plus, the weather's been shit for weeks."

"Man... sounds like some drinks in a foreign land is exactly what you need."

"For sure dude."

Mikey turned the music up a bit when the tracks changed. He bobbed his head a little and flexed his lips out. No more Ludacris. This was his jam now. I think I'd really appreciate electronic music like that if I was stoned, but I wasn't, so it was kind of annoying.

We passed through customs without any issues. That was the last time I ever got through Canadian customs without getting grilled. First left led us to White Rock and we pulled up to a liquor store.

"Let's grab a pint and walk the pier first," Mikey said.

"Sounds good man."

It was my first time walking into a liquor store. I'd never been in a bar before either—that would come later that evening—so the selection in the store was the largest I'd ever seen. I didn't know where to go at first, so I followed Mikey. He walked with purpose straight to the rum section and grabbed a pint of Captain Morgan. I was just glad it wasn't Bacardi 151. I was getting tired of that stuff.

I paid, and we hopped back in the car and drove down to a parking lot near the pier. I paid for the parking and we went for a walk. At this point it was getting dark and I was feeling hungry. There was a light mist from the ocean, swaying in the lamps that lit the pier. I could hear the waves clapping against the wooden posts of the pier.

We traded off taking pulls from the pint in its brown bag like hobos. We had one can of Coca-Cola. I took a gulp of that after my first few pulls but eventually the taste of spiced rum didn't bother me anymore. It was cold when we got there, typical November weather, but I started to feel warm as we wandered up and down the pier.

"Let's grab a bite to eat," I suggested.

"Yeah mang. Could use something before having more." The pint was finished, and Mikey dropped it in a trash can as we walked onto Marine Drive, with its assortment of bars and restaurants.

The *Charlie Don't Surf* sign stood out to me right away. *What an odd name for a restaurant.* I felt it must be a reference to *Apocalypse Now*, one of Robert Duvall's lines before that helicopter scene. "Let's go there!" Mikey nodded, and we walked in. Thinking of that movie always made me feel angry, even though I liked the story.

We were seated quickly. It was late on a weekday and the place wasn't very busy. I wanted a burger. I also wanted to class myself up a bit for the first drink I ever ordered at a restaurant. I settled on Sex on the Beach, because I'd heard about it once, I don't know where. Sounded very classy. Turned out to be disappointing, so I switched to Sleeman's Honey Brown after that. *Delicious*.

We scarfed our food like the fat boys we grew up as, barely a word exchanged other than passing napkins or ketchup for the fries. A few rounds of drinks and we paid our tabs separately. Things were fuzzy, and I stumbled once or twice when we exited.

Mikey led us down the drive a bit more on foot and we ended up in a place that seemed like a dance club but was empty. The guy at the entrance was the first man I'd seen that looked like a Canadian. I didn't know much about Canadians, just that they lived further north, which meant it was colder, they played hockey, put a leaf on their flag, and they had Bulwinkle, and Bret "The Hitman" Hart. I had this image in my mind that they were all larger fellas with beards, like lumberjacks or something. Except for Bret Hart; he was clean shaven but still a badass. Turns out they're basically the same as Washingtonians like me, but this one guy at the door had a short beard and was built like he could knock down a tree with his hands. He checked our IDs.

"You boys go to Western?"

"Oh yeah. Yeah, yeah, we do. How'd ya know?"

"Come on in. If you've got your student card, there's a discount on drinks." We walked past him and I couldn't help but notice how much Mikey was smiling. We were in the club. It was empty and they were going to give us cheap drinks because they knew us. We sat down and started pounding rum and Cokes.

***

The next thing I remember, we're at a Wendy's drive-thru on Samish Way, back in Bellingham, back in America. I mumbled and finally got out my order: Two Jr. Bacon Cheeseburgers, fries, and a Frosty. Mikey giggled and ordered his meal. I handed him cash, which is weird because I didn't have any on me when we left.

"Where the fuck… What the fuck happened man?"

"Dude, just be cool," Mikey snickered, "I can't believe we got back into the country."

We rolled up to Buchanan, parked, and then went to my place to eat our meals. Sitting down at the small coffee table in the living room, scarfing again, I nodded at the broken TV across the room. Mikey raised his eyebrows. "That's shitty man," he said.

"Yeah it is. AND SOMEONE STILL NEEDS TO REPLACE IT." I smacked the wall behind me.

"Shut the fuck up, Zach," came a reply from Travis's bedroom. My face erupted with heat.

"WHAT THE FUCK DID YOU SAY!?" I jumped up.

"Woah man. Take it easy." Kevin emerged from our bedroom.

"NO. THAT'S FUCKING BULLSHIT. HE BREAKS MY SHIT AND WON'T EVEN PAY FOR IT. FUCK YOU TRAVIS!" I yelled at the wall.

"Fuck you man." Travis slammed his door shut.

"I WILL FUCKING KILL YOU, YOU LITTLE BITCH!" Mikey scurried off with the remnants of his meal. Kevin got between me and Travis's door and started pushing me to our room.

"Just chill man. It's cool. Just chill." I heard some voices in Travis's room and then there was laughter.

"YOU THINK THIS IS FUCKING FUNNY!? COME OUT HERE ASSHOLE."

"No man. No. Come on. Be cool. You're drunk." Kevin was holding me back and pushing me towards our room. We got back to our room. Kevin closed the door.

"Oh my god, man." Kevin went to sit down at his desk. I never saw him lose his temper and I don't know if he had ever been around someone who had.

"I'm sorry man, but this is fucking bullshit."

I sat at my desk for a while, stewing and drunk, yelling insults at Travis periodically. I heard the suite door open. *Good. Fuck that guy. He better get out of here.* Then the door to our room opened and I was surprised to see two police officers walk in. *Shit.*

The officers separated Kevin and me, talking to each of us. Kevin was sober and kept repeating he had a test in the morning. Once the cop was done with him, he talked to Travis, who had not left the suite after all.

"When he threatened to kill you, did you think that was a legitimate threat? Were you afraid?" the officer asked him, sounding serious and official. Travis glanced at me.

"No sir. He's really drunk and pissed off, but I know he wouldn't actually try to kill me." I no longer cared about the TV. That lowballing, clumsy stoner took mercy upon me, the only reason my record reflects no crimes.

Despite Travis's statement, I was still arrested, as I was underage and drunk. I tried to explain that I drank legally, and the cops wanted to know how, and I thought about telling them Mikey and I went to Canada and he drove me back, but I knew Mikey was drunk and that would get him in trouble too. So, I dropped it and they cuffed me. We walked down the hall and out to a squad car parked in the front. I sat in the back. One of the cops took off, leaving this one to book me.

"Alright sir. Do you have anywhere that you can go tonight? Any friend close by? You can't go back here tonight. If you do, you're going straight to jail." *Holy shit. Are they letting me off? Were they just trying to scare me?* I remembered my friend John lived in the New England Apartments on Douglas Avenue, just a short drive away.

"My friend John lives over in the New England's."

"What's John's phone number?" I gave it to him and he called John, who eventually picked up.

"Hello is this John?... Yes, this is the Bellingham Police. We have one of your friends, a Zachary Neuhaus... Yes... He is drunk and under arrest. He can't go back to the dorms this evening. Can he stay at your place?... Alright. We will be over in a moment." He hung up.

"You're in luck, sir. Just remember, if I find out you went back to the dorms tonight, you will go to jail."

"Yes sir."

He started up the car and the radio came on. Christian Rock. *Is that the Newsboys?* I remembered them from all those mission trips I went on with the church. That seemed so long ago. I knew that somewhere there was probably a ton of people who thought this chubby, mustachioed cop was an instrument of God's will, that God was working through him somehow to reach out to me. I cried quietly in the backseat and the cop looked back with concern in his eyes. I hated myself so much.

40

Your Body is a Container

Location: Bellingham, WA
Age: 19

I woke up on John's floor and traipsed back home. As I walked in the front door of BT, a larger lady emerged from an office that I never noticed before.

"Are you Zach Neuhaus?" *Uh oh.*

"Uhhh yes. I'm Zach."

"Come on in for a minute." I followed her into her office. As I walked through the door I noticed her name and title. Her name was Sharon and she was the Resident Director I had been avoiding being referred to by Bethany. Instead I fucked up and referred myself.

"So, police were called last night because you were drunk and threatened to kill your suitemate. One of our R.A.'s went by due to the commotion but when she heard the death threat she thought it was unsafe, so she called the police."

"That makes sense."

"You're being trespassed from university residences."

"What does that mean?"

"It means that you will no longer be allowed to live on-campus and can also not enter any on-campus housing. You do not need to move out today. You can stay until the end of the quarter."

"Okay."

"Would you like to talk about what led to the events of last night?" I proceeded to overshare, but it didn't work on her like it had on Bethany.

"Are you feeling suicidal?"

"What? No. No, I've never thought of that. I just fucked up by being angry when I was drunk." The truth: I was. Not like put a gun in your mouth sort of suicidal. More like a slow suicidal. That's what my eating and drinking habits and the generally unhealthy way I lived my life were all about. And I hid it because I felt like I wasn't worth it and if you're convinced of that, you really don't want help. I didn't love myself. On some level I don't think I knew how.

"I don't think you're telling me everything. There's no judgment here. The only judgment you're going to get here has already been handed down by the university's judicial officer. He's the one that trespassed you. I'm just here to help. I want you to get good grades and be healthy." I wanted to trust her, but I couldn't figure out how to. I was trying to lift weights at the gym that were well past my max. It was exhausting.

"I don't know what else to say. I've been partying since freshmen year. My roommate broke my TV and wouldn't pay for it. I went to Canada and drank legally, then got heated back here and got arrested for drinking, which is strange."

"Your body is a container," she said matter-of-factly.

"What?"

"It doesn't matter that you drank in Canada. For what it's worth, I believe you drank in Canada. I also believe the cops found empty bottles of Bacardi 151 in your room. You didn't drink those last night, but you did drink them other times."

"Yeah, that's true." I must have missed the part where the cops swept the room.

"I think you're depressed and drinking a lot to try and cope with it. Are you aware that alcohol actually makes people more depressed? You're not a bad person for trying that, lots have, but you should know that it will never ever work."

"Okay. Can I go now?"

"Oh. Yeah. Sure." I got up to leave.

"One last thing." She walked around the table to meet me as I walked out, "I'm sure you're going to have some legal issues because of what happened. There is a legal center on campus that provides referrals to local lawyers who provide free consultations to students. Also, you should talk to your family about what happened and consider going to therapy. There's nothing wrong with going." She handed me a brochure.

"Thanks." I left. I went back to my room and slept the rest of the day.

41

Scam

Location: Bellingham, WA
Age: 19

I didn't go to class the next few days. I didn't eat much either. Lying in bed, watching *The Boondocks* and *Family Guy* was about all I could do. I don't think I even showered.

A letter arrived in the mail from the Bellingham PD. I was formally charged with Minor in Possession (Alcohol) and Disorderly Conduct. They could have also charged with me a low-degree assault, but Travis' statement had prevented that. I'm glad I didn't make him afraid. There was a court date the first week of December.

I found the hours for the legal info center online and decided to check it out. A woman that I would briefly date a year and a half later was the only staff on hand. She gave me a list of the law firms that did free consults and then put me out of her mind completely. I called one up, then walked over to their office.

It turned out the whole thing was a scam for them to lure in some business. I heard about it later. They gave free consults for a half hour and then made it sound like the consequences you were facing "could" be heavy, but with their help it could be handled. I was in a bad place and fell for it, only to show up on my court date like a schmuck as the only M.I.P. case with a paid lawyer. The other nine college students just plead guilty and got the same sentence I did. Three hundred bucks down the drain for some small-city leech that needed billable hours. About the only thing I prided myself on at that point was being smart and I was failing at that. *Why did I fall for this? I should have known better. I shouldn't have trusted this lawyer from the start. I got his name from the university. I know better than trusting officialdom. They're just another type of authority.*

The court gave me a fine, required I take an alcohol class, and sentenced me to ten hours of community service. I told the judge I was moving home after that quarter. I'd decided to drop out and sort my life out. He said it was fine and that I wouldn't be required to appear again, so long as I sent the necessary paperwork up promptly.

42

The Old Man

Location: Greater Seattle Area
Age: 20

It was a rainy day when I started community service. Puddles on the pavement made splashing noises as my '92 Honda Civic rolled through the parking lot. I parked and stepped out and looked with despair upon where I was to spend four hours that day. It was about how I imagined buildings to look in communist countries; the large faded blue sign with "GOODWILL" written in white, pinned against a dull gray wall, with twin pillars of concrete marking the entrance, old discarded items stored within like the retail version of a soup kitchen. *This is probably where everyone would shop if we were communists* and I was thankful we weren't.

I was to work with a more diverse cohort than I had since my days at McDonald's. There were only two groups back then, white teens and Hispanic cooks.

At Goodwill there were four groups, maybe more. There was an assortment of Asians, some that I thought were Filipino, a couple of Russians, two Muslim women who never spoke and stayed together always, and one old black man with freckles on his nose. I felt out of place.

My job for the next four hours was to take new donations and distribute them to appropriate sections of the store. I was then to organize them in a manner that was enticing to customers. The only similar skill I had was taking new movies out of boxes and placing them in high traffic areas at Blockbuster, where I'd been working for a month. Everyone wanted those movies though. I'd never had to place items that others had literally given away. *How can you convince people to buy things that were thrown away?* The only people that I knew who shopped at Goodwill were proto-hipsters, kids who behaved too well and had too good of grades to be convincing as punk or goth or grunge. We just didn't have a word for them yet, but today I know they're hipsters. *What items would they want? Suspenders, corduroy pants, maybe some tacky jewelry?*

When I got to the unloading area in the back of the store, I was surprised by the lack of clothing. No clothing at all, just box after box of someone else's dishes. The Russians grabbed a box each, but the bottom of one of the boxes broke and dishes crashed to the ground, making a mess. The tired-looking man with a bulbous nose said something I didn't understand, then grabbed a different box and marched away. The old black man approached with a broom.

"Now that's no good," he remarked as he swept the broken dishes, "You got to grab at the bottom. Some of the boxes are soggy from sitting out here too long." I nodded at him and did as he said, then marched off to find the Russians. I didn't know where the dish section was but figured they did.

I caught up with them and we put our boxes down next to some old silverware that was tarnished and definitely not made of silver.

Then we trudged back to the loading area, no words exchanged, and grabbed more boxes. The Russians were all grabbing the boxes as the old black man said, though they never looked at him and acted like he wasn't there. I peeked at him whenever I got back there. He would be sweeping and then slowly bending down to pick up big pieces and shuffling like a grandpa over to the garbage. I assumed we were all here for community service and wondered what an old man like him must have done.

It was the fifth or sixth trip with the dishes, with the boxes stacked high by the old silverware, that the Russians broke off and sped for the exit. I stood there confused for a moment. One looked back and smiled and waved, saying something that I didn't understand. They did some brief paperwork, then left. *That must have been the last of their community service.* There were only a few boxes left in the loading area, so I returned to grab the last of them. The old man was no longer back there, so I took a five-minute break, then started back at the boxes.

My arms were feeling weak by the time I got the last box out of there. It was arm day at the gym two days before and I might have overdone it. As I set the last box down next to the rest, the old man walked up and began taking dishes out and laying them on the table. He'd lay out a row of dishes that looked similar to each other, then pull out more. He made some old man grunt-type noises, but otherwise not a peep. With each dish he would pause and look it over, then put it on top of or underneath the dish it was most like. The finest dishes, relatively speaking, were always on top. He had a system. I tried to copy him on the neighboring table.

We went on like that for a half hour or so, laying out rows of dishes, him at the table next to the stacked boxes, and me walking back and forth to grab more dishes for my table. Each time I passed him, I noticed something more about the old man. He wore black slacks, faded and a little wrinkled towards the bottom of the legs, a brown belt, with the end of the leather bent in an unintended way, and a blue long-sleeved, heavy polo shirt, that seemed brand new. He had a black watch, nothing fancy, and completed his ensemble with a pair of black shoes with two Velcro straps atop each foot, like the ones I had seen old men wearing at the nursing home my Nana died in. He smelled vaguely of tobacco, the type that one tastes in the mouth and doesn't inhale.

"Never seen a black man before?" He looked up while I was daydreaming about him smoking a pipe on a davenport, watching *Murder She Wrote*, the show Nana liked. I assumed all old people did similar things.

"Oh... sorry. Didn't mean to stare at you."

"It's alright." He smiled like an old man, not like a crook. I resumed stacking dishes.

"So, what are you in for?" He brought some dishes over to my table. I glanced over. His table was full. *Old man works fast.*

"Hmmm?"

"Oh... I got caught drinking."

"Why'd you do that?" He spoke without judgment, in a calm, knowing tone, like he was driving to a point, but not being mean about it. I imagined this is what my grandfathers would have sounded like, if I'd ever had one.

"It's a long story."

"Well you've got a long time. Haven't seen you here before. They give you ten hours?" He asked.

"Yeah. How'd you know?"

"Oh, you're not the first young man to come through here for that."

"What about you? What did you do?"

"Nothing," he looked up, "I just come here to help out." I felt immediately racist. *The Russians, Asians, Muslims, and the old black man, are they all employees or volunteers? Am I the only lawbreaker here?*

"I... sorry about that. I thought everyone was here for community service. I shouldn't have assumed you'd broken the law," I said sheepishly.

"Ha ha ha." He chuckled at my white anxiety. "It's okay."

"Okay."

"But why have you been drinking? You're a good-looking kid. Why don't you have a girlfriend and go to the movies and have fun that way?"

"Oh, I do. I mean, I've tried to. Sometimes it works out."

"Look. No man bats a thousand with women. Believe me. Ha ha."

"I know, I know."

"Can't beat yourself up about it. A woman broke your heart, is that why you drank?" His eyes were soft.

"No, I just need to drink to be around them."

"Nervous huh?" I thought of the doctor, the one that told me it was all stage fright.

"Not quite. I mean sometimes I'm shy, sure, but that's not what it is. I need it to... you know." I didn't want to spell it out.

"What are you talking about?" He stopped stacking and looked at me again. I could feel him looking at me and didn't want to look back. I wanted to scream at him and die at the same time. I felt naked.

"I can't be with them when I'm sober. I just... ya know... I need to use the bathroom." I walked away, down an aisle, past the Asians folding clothes, to the men's room. It was the first time I slipped up and let part of the truth out.

I locked a stall door behind me, then nearly puked when I saw someone's leftover diarrhea. *Oh god.* I lifted my foot and pressed the lever to send that nastiness away. Then I stood there, in the stink of a rude person who probably hadn't broken the law and thought a while. It was all coming back to me. I couldn't hold these memories in the back of my mind anymore.

"We just don't love each other anymore." Papa drunk and distant. Sitting in that decrepit bedroom, watching sports when he should have been watching his fucking kids. His great friend, Bobby. "Uncle" Bobby. The rhythmic slapping noise and heavy breathing. The pool. The Chinese restaurant. That bathroom with the floral pattern on the floor. Sitting on his lap so he could "read to me." THE CLOSET. That bastard. The doctor. My blood on a latex glove. Nonchalant and sterile, like hurting boys is routine. The kids at school. The first time I got aroused was against my will. The green dumpster and my wet pant leg. Greetings. That fucking Tyrant who was cruel and worthless except for that one time an adult tried to touch my dick at scout camp. My shorts pulled down in front of a hundred boys and men. Juan and his singing and that idiot shift supervisor. Being trapped. Crying on a curb. Wanting to die. *The inhaler. I almost did it.*

The outer bathroom door opened, and I heard the short shuffle steps only old people make. I wiped the sweat from my forehead. My heart was racing. There was a gentle knock on the stall door. I didn't know how long I'd been gone.

"You okay in there?"

"Not really. No. Not really."

"It's okay. Come on out." I hesitated, then opened the door.

"What was that about?" And the look on his face wrecked me. That old wrinkled, freckled face, and the look of concern. I couldn't breathe.

"It's okay. Just take it easy. You're alright." The old man motioned me over to a bench by the sink. We sat down on it. I hunched forward, my face in my hands. I was so ashamed.

"… I'm sorry." I sniffled.

"What? Why are you sorry? You haven't done anything wrong."

"I know. I just. I don't know." I cried. And I wasn't doing pretty crying, where there're just tears. No, I was doing that deep breath, gulping sort of pathetic crying. And then I was crying like Russell Crowe in *Gladiator*. That part with the snot when he finds his dead wife and son. The snot was going everywhere on my hands. I sniffled loud. The old man got up and I thought maybe he left me, but he shuffled back and handed me some paper towels. Feeling embarrassed, I took them and wiped my hands and face.

"Oh man." I sat up and took a deep breath.

"You're carrying an awful lot, don't you think?"

"Yeah. I am. I just don't know what to do. I want to be with a woman more than anything else. I want to be in love. I might even try marriage, though my family hasn't been very good at it."

"You just can't do it? Can't go to bed with them?"

"I try but I freak out unless I'm drunk or stoned. If they touch me it just doesn't work." I tilted my head up to see his response. His eyebrows were raised and his eyes had a shimmer that was absent before.

"Did someone hurt you? I don't mean a woman. I mean did someone hurt you when you were a boy?" He put his hand on my shoulder.

"...Yes." I leaned back down.

"Catholic?"

"Huh?

"Are you Catholic?"

"Uh, no. Presbyterian back when I went."

"Doesn't matter. This happens to a lot of boys, ya know? It just isn't talked about."

"That's the problem."

"THAT *is* the problem. It's a prison. All men feel pain. Why are we supposed to go through life lying about what we've felt, pretending everything is fine?"

"I don't know. I just feel so ashamed."

"Don't. It's not your fault. I don't know what to do except... I've seen an awful lot of men become alcoholics and drink themselves to early graves because they couldn't find a way to heal. Does that sound at all like how you got in trouble?"

"Yeah."

"What's your name?"

"Zach."

"James. Zach, they're never going to say sorry and they're probably never going to get punished. It's just probably not in the cards. I'm sorry. The only thing you can do to get back at them is find a way to live a healthy life and be happy. And the only way you're going to do that is if you get off the track you're on and stop hurting yourself. It's going to be hard before it gets easy. It might never get easy. But I bet it'll be easier than this."

It occurred to me then, on that bathroom bench, with an old man I just met, that I was getting more fatherly direction and care in that moment than I had from my biological father and stepfather combined my entire life. I was crushed that they hadn't cared more and liberated by the fact that some stranger had. And I'll admit I cried in front of that stranger for quite a while.

43

Mask off, Mask on

Location: Greater Seattle Area & Bellingham, WA
Age: 20

I went back and saw James one more time. For my second stint of community service, they let me stretch it out to six hours, so I wouldn't have to come back a third time. I learned more about him. He was a grandfather and he came to Goodwill to work on the days he didn't see his grandkids. Their mother worked, and he would pick them up from school when she was on the late shift.

James and I worked together and talked a lot more, this time while hanging donated clothes. He wanted to make sure I hadn't been drinking and kept reiterating to me that I should see a shrink. "There's no shame in it. You can't fix a broken leg without a doctor, right?" I've never broken a bone, but I knew what he meant.

I was still worried about women though. I worried that men would judge me, but worse than that, by far, was what women

224

would think. Would they think I was confused or girly or gay? What if they wanted the strong, silent type that soldiers on, with no cracks in his armor? Did John Wayne ever cry around his wife? *Why the fuck do I care what John Wayne did?*

It got towards the end of the day. James and I walked to the back to see if there were any last-minute donations. I had learned to walk slow with old people, from walking with Nana up and down the pews, all those times she tortured me by taking me to old woman church. I don't think all elders should be respected, but the Nanas and James's of the world definitely should be.

"Looks like we're all finished up," James said near the end.

"I've got a few minutes left I think." We sat down on some chairs that had been donated but deemed unworthy of re-sale. They were partially broken, but still sturdy enough to sit on.

"James, I'm still not sure about the women."

"How so?"

"I'm not the strong, silent type. I can be stoic in public, but behind closed doors I just know I'm going to be mushy."

"Ahhhh. You're worried that if you let them in they won't like what they find."

"Yeah."

"Well, look, I suppose if all you do all day is cry about your feelings, then yeah, maybe they will. Same time, if a woman spends all day doing nothing but crying about her feelings, most men would leave too."

"Yeah."

"But if you open up and share your feelings with them and there's more to you than just that, why would they leave? It's about balance. You tell them about this stuff that hurts you, that happened when you were a kid, maybe you cry some, and they comfort you, and then a few hours later, you and her are having dinner and then on the couch watching a movie or something, the usual couple stuff, and when you go to bed with her, you're able to

225

make it work now because you trust her. Maybe she'll know that's why and so she'll trust you more because you trust her. And then she'll open up more and the whole relationship will become better."

"That makes sense. I still worry that it would be unexpected, like she'd think it wasn't normal."

"Just because something is unexpected or abnormal does not mean it is wrong. Let me tell you, I can see a woman leaving a guy if all he does is cry. I've never heard of that happening, but I can imagine it. But what I have seen is a lot of men getting divorced because they stopped connecting on an emotional level. My ex-wife said I never opened up. You might not realize it because you're so young and inexperienced, but women have been begging for us to be vulnerable for a while now."

And that was how it was with James and I. We parted ways a few minutes later and I haven't seen him since. I went back to that store a few years later, pretending to be a shopper, still feeling very white and out of place, and he wasn't there. He was rather old, so it's possible he has passed on. If not, I like to imagine he's splitting his time between playing with his grandkids and doling out fatherly advice to errant young men who never got any from their own fathers.

***

I went back to Western the following Fall Quarter. I wrote an admissions essay about drinking and family that might have been too honest. My last two years there, I had a few girlfriends and several flings, and we slept in the same bed, but didn't have sex. I didn't even try to. This confused them and I made up excuses. The most confused was the one that woke up while I was yelling in my sleep. That night had been the only time I ever watched

226

Deliverance. Another one noticed that I must search my closet before going to bed at night.

"Was someone hiding in it once?" She asked. Women figure things out quickly, it seems.

I did have sex with one woman, towards the end, but I was drunk. Very drunk.

My friends thought I was a player because I kissed a lot of women at parties. They heard noises coming from my bedroom and assumed lots of sex was happening. I'd use my hands and mouth. Making a woman orgasm is an effective way to avoid sex some of the time. A lot of them fall asleep afterwards, just like those stereotypes about men. But some are energized by orgasms, which I never understood, and they become enthusiastic about returning the favor. Those were the nights my plan backfired, and I'd let them jerk me off with lube while my heart was fluttering, and legs were shaking. I passed out twice. Or I'd drink a bunch and brush my teeth before they came over. Then we'd go down on each other, the woman none the wiser. The energized ones I quickly broke up with. I couldn't sustain alcohol or panic at that frequency and still have perfect grades, which I told myself I needed due to my previous failures.

I could have just avoided women altogether, but I was in a bit of an ego trap. I am decent looking enough to attract some women. I'm also a nerd who didn't really "get any" in high school. If I don't show an interest in the women I have opportunities with now, it leads to questions. Am I still religious? No. Am I gay? No. Is something else wrong with me? Yeah, and I don't want to talk about it because deep down inside I think I deserved it somehow and don't love myself as a result. And when you don't love yourself, you don't want to get better. Even after James, I still felt this way for many years. His message had to marinate in my pain before I could eat it.

I let my friends believe I was a womanizer. It was easier than telling them the truth. I don't like who I was back then. Some of the women just wanted me because of how I looked, but some of them were nice, considerate types who would have made a good partner. I could have chosen to trust them, but I didn't feel like I could. I still felt ashamed. I pushed woman after woman out of my life without adequate explanation, which likely made them feel used.

Then, I graduated in June 2008. The economy was shit. And I accepted a job overseas that I was totally unqualified for.

44

Pizza Weekends

Location: Busan, Republic of Korea
(Southeast coast of South Korea)
Age: 22-23

"I'm sorry," I said with a muffled voice, my face in the pillow.
"It's okay, Zach," she said back to me.

"I'm sorry. I really want it to work."

"You're being too hard on yourself. Really, it's okay." She wrapped an arm around my head and hugged me. We were naked in bed together in her little apartment in Busan.

It's 2008, the Great Recession, and I've traveled to the other side of the world for work, as an English teacher in South Korea. I lucked out and got to date a sweet, understanding woman from Australia, who was teaching in the same city. I don't think it's fair that women often end up providing therapy for the men in their lives, but I'm grateful this one was willing to. I didn't tell her specifically what had happened to me, only making vague

229

references to a "difficult childhood," but I think she understood. She wouldn't have been the first woman to figure it out.

She was the first person I had sex with while sober and it took some time for me to get there. But her reassurance and patience led me to trust her and we were able to make it work. She's the only woman I've ever loved.

"Come on, let's have some pizza," she said, getting out of bed and walking across the hardwood floor to the small table in the middle of the room. I was skeptical of Korean pizza at first, the sweet potato and corn and white drizzle. I'm pretty sure some of it had spam. But I came to love it, and it was a staple of our weekends together.

"That sounds good," I replied, lifting my head from the pillow. Food could always put me in a better mood. She put some slices on a plate and came back to bed. Sitting back down, she leaned over and gave me a kiss on the cheek.

"I love you," she said, and her eyes told me she meant it. It nearly wrecked me again. I still didn't think I deserved to be loved.

"I love you, too." And then I took a big bite of that sweet-potato-covered pizza. She picked up the controller for the D.V.D. player and pressed play. McDreamy was doing something important on screen.

Sometimes we'd take the train to Seoul or walk along Haeundae Beach for hours. Other times we'd cozy up together at her place or mine and eat Korean pizza for lunch and dinner, and kimchi bo-com-bop (fried rice) for breakfast. She'd always want to watch Grey's Anatomy, which I pretended to not like. And once we got past my issues, there was a lot of sex and a level of true intimacy I'd never had before.

We traveled to China and the Philippines together, and all-over South Korea. She always held my hand, covered in sweat, during takeoffs and landings or anytime the plane moved in a manner I didn't anticipate.

We broke up at Incheon Airport, September 2009. At that point, I don't think we were in love anymore. I think we were a comfort to each other, two foreigners trying to make our way in a beautiful but strange land during the worst economic downturn of our young lives. She went back to Australia to work at her parents restaurant. And I went back to America, to wallow between contract jobs and unemployment and resolve some unfinished business with my family.

When I die, I'll remember her and the time we spent together. It will make me smile and remember how my life slowly turned around. It wasn't a quick u-turn though.

She was the first person I ever trusted sexually. That changed sex for me. With a few exceptions, I could do it sober now. I thought I was "cured." I mourned our relationship for a few months back in America, but after that I started chasing. The next five years were filled with flings, casual arrangements, brief monogamies, and even a few one-night stands. I told myself to be transparent about my intentions and none of my partners ever complained about being led on, though I imagine they wouldn't even if they had been.

45

The Sterile Scent of Death

Location: Greater Seattle Area
Age: 24

"**A**lright, Zachariah," Papa said. "Let's get out of here."
"What?" I replied.

"I'm tired of this place," he continued. "Let's go back to the apartment."

"Oh... Papa. You can't leave."

"WHAT? Sure, I can," he said, struggling back and forth in the hospital bed, trying to sit up. But he had no strength left and couldn't manage even that.

"Stop it. You're too sick for this. You need to stay here," I implored, my voice cracking a little.

"Okay. Okay." He gave up, laying back down, glassy eyes staring at the ceiling. He exhaled and slowly ran his tubeless hand over his light blue hospital gown. *I don't think the nurses shave his face.* A few minutes passed. Then he started again.

"When I'm feeling better, we're going to get out of here and grab some Mexican food at *La Fogata*. Then we can watch the Mariners back at my place." It was the type of declaration that insists on confirmation for the sake of comfort.

"That'll be fun, Papa. I went to *La Fogata* the other day and they asked about you." It was his regular haunt, since he moved to an apartment in Maple Valley, by way of a retirement home he found too restrictive. The restaurant was just across the street and he went there every night to drink vodka and occasionally help a waitress with her bills. I tried to stop that last part, but Papa proved incorrigible.

"Where is my van? They park it here?" he continued.

"Sarah's taking care of it for you. She got it washed yesterday." I lied to the dying man. I didn't know how to tell him that his apartment was vacated, and his van was sold. The doctors said it was just a matter of time. Parts of his insides had been removed and all he could keep down was Ensure shakes.

I hated being in hospitals. They were even worse than the doctor's office. The sterile scent of death is more convincing here. I felt like a pet at the vet, wanting to whimper and run away, because I knew what was lurking down that hall. *Why do I always have to smell everything?*

I'd never seen Papa any way other than obese. Now he looked like the Jews I'd seen in documentaries about the Holocaust. I've always watched a lot of documentaries and that was the first thing I thought when I saw him after he collapsed. Shriveled up to almost nothing, just skin hanging on bones. *Cancer. What a way to go.*

I tried to not think much about my father. Everything about him and our relationship depressed me, angered me. For much of my life I had felt worthless, like the distance and neglect and empty words were what I had deserved, as well as the predation and pain that arrived in that vacuum. And I blamed him for it. It is odd to feel a sense of obligation to someone you resent. To have sincere, familial feelings for someone who hurt you so much. To care for one who didn't care about you. *He was never there like a parent should be. He failed me so much. He thought I was dumb enough to survive on lip service, like telling me "I love you" was all I needed. He has seven kids from three marriages and is universally considered a bad dad. Yet here I am, dutifully comforting him while he dies. Why?* But I couldn't help but feel terrible for him. And I hoped that when it was my time, people would visit me in the hospital, even if I didn't deserve it. So, I stayed a while, and lied to him some more.

"Are the Mariners going to make the playoffs this year, you think?" Papa broke the silence.

"Oh, I bet we will, Papa. Looking good so far. It's been a while. I think we're due." Papa smiled. I hadn't watched baseball or basketball in years, only football. I was too busy drinking and trying to find anything other than contract work.

It was 2010 and I was 24 years old. The Great Recession wasn't kind to PoliSci majors like me. Papa was now 84 and his decade-long rebellion against medical advice had finally caught up with him. There is no telling how long he could have gone if he had just listened a little to the doctors when they "lectured" him about his lifestyle. But he resented all of it, I'm not quite sure why, and refused to see doctors or even go near their offices, unless it was to refill a prescription. When they told him he was out of refills, he would call their offices. And when they seized that opportunity to try and schedule an appointment to see how he was doing, he would dismiss it out of hand and issue an ultimatum: either allow more refills or I'll just die. I guess he sounded convincing.

A nurse peeked his head in the room.

"Hello Forrest," he said cheerfully. "How are you feeling?"

"Oh, I'm alright. My son and I were just talking about grabbing some Mexican food after this," Papa replied. The nurse entered the room and proceeded to check the bag connected to Papa's hand. It was full of clear liquid.

"That sounds like fun," the nurse said. "I love nachos."

"Mmmmm" Papa hummed and nodded his agreement. He was lying now too. He didn't eat at the Mexican restaurants. He survived on vodka.

"Any discomfort at all?" the nurse asked.

"Oh no. No. I'm alright. Just hoping to get out of here soon." Papa glanced at the ceiling again.

The nurse looked at me. I looked back with a look that was familiar to him.

"Well, I'm sure when you're feeling better, your son can drive you home," he lied along with me and Papa. Everyone was lying now.

"Yep," I quickly said. Papa silently nodded. His eyes were watery more than before as he stared at the ceiling.

"Okay. Well, I'll check back on you this evening. Let us know if you need anything," the nurse said while walking out the door.

More moments of silence followed after the nurse departed. We sat there in the sterile scent of death and waited. I thought about life and how it ends and how much time we don't have. Looking at Papa, as he stared at the ceiling, perhaps looking for his God, I realized it wouldn't be very long for me. I never thought I would be immortal, but like most young people I had put off thoughts of death because it seemed so far away. *Papa probably felt the same way once, and now look at him. And young people die all the time.* One of my childhood friends – one of the most beautiful souls I'd ever known – had been shot and killed the year before, while I was vacationing in Beijing. It was unpleasant to think about how soon this all ends, and I tried to swerve away, but I couldn't fight my mind while sober. It's relentless.

Papa must have been pondering things, too.

"Dammit," he suddenly said, frustrated, as his eyes overflowed, and he reached up with his tubeless hand to swipe away tears. I got up and grabbed some tissues.

"It's okay, Papa," I lied as I handed them to him. *It will all be over soon.*

But it wasn't. Papa continued to defy medical experts. He survived the hospital, albeit in a gravely diminished state, and they moved him to a hospice facility, and he outlived every other patient there.

46

The Only Catholic President We've Had

Location: Greater Seattle Area
Age: 24

I visited Papa several more times in the hospital and at the hospice facility he went to afterwards. My visits were one-part duty, but I had selfish reasons also. I couldn't help but desire answers to provide context for the raw pain of childhood memories. I was seeking closure, regardless of what those answers might be. I would rather know than not.

On one such visit, I decided to find out for certain how much he had known about Uncle Bobby. It was the last issue I needed to raise with him, having already discussed the divorce, among other things. I'd been putting this one off for a while, but he was deteriorating, and I didn't know if I would get another chance.

The hospice facility was much smaller than a hospital or even a doctor's office. In other circumstances, it could have easily functioned as a small restaurant or café. On a cloudy winter day, I pulled up in my 1992 blue Honda Civic, parked, and walked inside.

"Hello," said a cheerful nurse as I walked in.

"Hello. I'm here to see Forrest Neuhaus."

"Oh good. He's awake and right over there," she pointed to a bed with a shriveled up bald man in it. My mind rebelled whenever I saw him now. He was no longer my fat old father.

Don't stare, I reminded myself as I walked past the other patients. Some were asleep, some awake. The sleeping ones slept like they were already dead, curled up in the fetal position, like a baby resting in its mother's arms one last time. *Hopeful to the last*, I suppose. The awake ones were usually staring at the wall or out the window, time passing by, resigned to their fates. There were eight of them, all in varying stages of death. All past the point of no return. *But aren't we all?*

It was eerily quiet, save for the sound of petite nurses moseying and the slow, labored breathing of the dying. The sterile scent of death was different here, less pink soap and more cough. I could feel it in my nose like an incipient sinus infection you feel one cold morning. I imagined I was catching some sickness every time I was there.

Papa was facing away from the entrance and hadn't noticed me walking towards him. He was awake though.

"Hey Papa," I said in a lower tone to avoid startling him.

"Oh! Zachariah," he said, with a smile. His yellow, misshapen teeth seemed almost rotten. The hue was more brown than yellow. There had always been a few missing, but it looked like more were gone now.

"How are you feeling?" I asked.

238

"They say I'm on my way out. But they've been saying that for months," Papa replied defiantly. There was no more self-pitying like in the hospital. No more broken dams flooding down his face.

"Well, don't worry about that, Papa. If it happens, it happens."

"Right," Papa replied, then with a smirk, "You think they have a spot ready for me next to the high school?" He was his old, dark-humored self again.

"Well, yes, but there is an issue," I played along.

"Oh?"

"Yes. Unfortunately, it seems that the officers are requiring space at a higher volume than expected. So, well, I am sad to inform you that they will bury you next to the enlisted."

"Oh heavens!" Papa exclaimed. He put his hands to his mouth.

I laughed. He laughed. A few minutes passed. It started to rain outside, a gentle pitter-patter on the roof.

"You know, I really wouldn't care," he said.

"What?"

"The enlisted. That's where I started anyways. Started enlisted and retired an officer. Worked my way up."

"Oh. I don't know if they even separate them by rank. I haven't been there since Cub Scouts," I confessed.

"Well... you shall have plenty of opportunities in the future," Papa chuckled.

"I suppose so."

"I will have some of them court martialed in the afterlife though," Papa said.

"What for?"

"FOR DEFYING MY DIRECT ORDERS!" Papa yelled. One of his sleeping co-occupants stirred and sat up.

"Sorry," I said to the dying man next to us. He laid back down.

"How many times have I yelled for them to save me a spot?" Papa quizzed me, officially.

"Oh, you see the problem is that the officers all outrank you. So, the enlisted were the only ones listening. The sergeants saved you a spot."

"Ha! Figures," Papa seemed content in his rumination.

One of the nurses, the shortest of the petite, came by with an Ensure shake.

"How are you feeling, Frosty?" she asked.

"Oh, I'm holding up."

"I brought you a shake. Are you hungry at all?"

"Sure," he said, then, "Hey, have you met my son?"

Here we go.

"Oh, no I haven't," she smiled and extended her hand. I stood up and shook it. I can't remember her name, but I told her mine.

Papa took the Ensure shake and sipped at it as the nurse walked away. I sat back down.

"Why do you have to do that?" I asked.

"Whatever do you mean?"

"I'm not here looking for someone."

"Oh. I don't know what you're talking about. The Ori*ntals are pretty nice though. Very friendly." A few beds away, a different nurse paused what she was doing, registering the comment.

"Just because I dated one, doesn't mean I'm going to date all of them," I said.

"You sure?"

"Yes," I snickered, "It's not like an addiction or something. I've dated white women and even one African-American."

"Really? A black girl?" Papa was surprised.

"Yeah. That was a while ago. You don't... have a problem with that sort of thing, do you?" I asked, peering at him, officially.

"What? Of course not. I voted for Kennedy!" Papa defended himself. I laughed.

"What the hell does that have to do with it?" I teased.

"The Kennedys were well liked by that community."

"Yeah, when they weren't spying on 'em."

"WHAT?" Papa yelled. The dying man next to us had just gone back to sleep and stirred again.

"Keep your voice down," I whispered aggressively.

"I just can't believe you came here to bad mouth the only Catholic president we've had," Papa whispered aggressively back at me.

I couldn't help but laugh. The dying man opened his eyes and stared at the ceiling, as if he wanted it to all be over at this moment. The shortest of the petite walked by and offered him an Ensure shake. He shook his head "no" and then closed his eyes again. She looked at me.

"I'm sorry," I whispered to her. She smiled with her mouth but not her eyes and continued to the next bed.

"See? They're Catholic too. You are hurting your chances," Papa informed me. I struggled to contain my laughter.

"Please stop," I said.

"Oh, alright."

A few moments passed. It was still raining outside, harder now than before. I wondered how long my father would last. And I felt badly about coming, despite our conversations. I didn't like it and didn't want to anymore. All things considered, I had gone well past my obligations. *Why did I come today*? Then I remembered. *One last matter to discuss.*

"Papa, do you remember Uncle Bobby?" I asked.

"Bobby? Yeah. He hasn't even come by to visit or anything."

"You're still in touch?"

"Not in a while. Figured he would have at least called when I was in the hospital though." Papa frowned.

"Rich guys," I shook my head, knowingly.

"Yeah," Papa agreed.

"When was the last time you talked?"

"Oh… let me see," Papa gazed at the ceiling. "We spoke a couple times after he won the lotto. And I feel like there was another time right around when the Seahawks were in the Super Bowl against the Steelers."

"Tough game," I said.

"Yeah," Papa let out a sigh. "I wish I coulda seen the M's or them win once." He didn't live long enough to see the Seahawks win the Super Bowl. I might not live long enough to see the Mariners win the World Series.

"Did he actually win the lotto?" I asked.

"Yes."

"Hmmmm," I pondered that. *He's either very committed to the lie or Bobby actually won the lotto. I suppose that's of secondary importance though.*

"Do you remember when Mom tried to make him stop coming around?"

"Oh…yeah. She was a bit hysterical," Papa shrugged, dismissively.

"What was that all about? I vaguely recall her yelling at you on the phone one time about him." It was a lie of omission. But I had to know for certain that Papa did not love me.

"Your mother never liked Bobby. And she didn't like that once we were divorced I could do what I wanted. You see, divorce is the big one and once they go through with it, what more do they have to threaten you with?" Papa explained.

"Child support, I guess."

"She didn't want to reduce me like that. We had our disagreements, but she agreed to less money than the court offered." *I knew that already.*

"I don't think she was trying to control you. I think she just didn't like Bobby for some reason," I leaned forward.

"Why the hell not?" Papa asked.

"You didn't think it was weird, the interest he took in us?" I peered at Papa, accusing him with narrowed eyes.

"You and Sarah?" He sounded nervous, with a wavering voice, and avoided my eyes.

"Yeah. Does that seem like normal behavior for a man?" I inquired, officially.

"What do you mean? What's wrong with my friend playing with the kids?" Papa sounded defensive.

"Did he ever come by when we weren't there?"

A moment passed. Papa looked away and bit at his lower lip. Then he reluctantly met my eyes.

"Did Uncle Bobby ever come by when your children weren't there?" I asked again, from the back of the throat. Papa's eyes showed recognition I had never seen from him before. Sadness, too. *You know exactly what I'm talking about.*

"I don't think so," Papa confessed. He broke eye contact. He rolled his lips against themselves.

"What do you think about that?" My left knee hopped anxiously. I was almost to the information I needed.

"I just... I wish your mother wouldn't have blown things out of proportion. He was one of my only friends." *And now I know.* It crushed me that he was denying me an apology or even a verbal recognition of his negligence. There were many failed parental moments in my history with him, but I hadn't felt stung like this since the day I confirmed my suspicions about Christmas presents. And this stung a hell of a lot worse. I looked away and pretended to check out a nurse as she walked by. My eyes were teary though. I couldn't have looked at her ass if I wanted to.

"Heh heh," Papa chuckled, knowingly.

"Yeah," I agreed about the ass I couldn't see. More silence followed as I regained my composure. *Don't let him see.* There was a break in the rain. I took it as my sign to leave.

"Well, Papa," I said, "I've got to be going. It was good seeing you."

"You too, Zachariah."

I got up and began slowly walking away. The shortest of the petite walked by me. She smiled with her mouth and eyes this time, like she'd forgiven me for disturbing the dying man. I turned back.

"Papa."

"Yes?"

"I don't think they like that."

"Like what?"

"Being called Ori*ntal."

"Oh, come on," Papa scoffed and turned away. And that's how I left him. He was a defiant and selfish old man. I no longer saw anything redeeming about him.

I walked to the car and got inside, then sat there for a moment. *This is the end*, I thought, then tried to talk myself out of it. *He's my father and he's scared. No. I can't keep letting people off when they hurt me. I know he had a hard childhood, but he doesn't deserve my love. Not after everything that's happened. Every time I visit, I end up feeling like this. Where are his other kids?* And it was the end. I drove away and never saw him again. I didn't call either. He was already dead to me.

***

I got a temporary job managing the re-election campaign of a state legislator. A few months passed, then summer arrived. That's when he finally died. I didn't attend the funeral, but still ended up with his casket flag. Apparently, Mom had insisted that I get it. Even in the end, she very much wanted me to have a good father. And the woman with the sad smile still couldn't know what one looked like.

And how did I feel on June 30th of 2010 when I got the phone call from my solemn-sounding mother? I felt nothing for several hours, until I got home from work late that night. Then I poured myself a shot of Smirnoff to remember him, drank it down, started crying, had another, and another, and another, and then wrote this:

I hated him, and I loved him. I wanted him to die and was sad to see him leaving, because his leaving reminded me of all I'd lost and was going to lose. Mostly, I just wanted it to be over and felt relieved when it was. He was my father, though he was certainly not much of one.

My father's death was another turning point for me. I was beginning to question the negative core beliefs I had about myself. His intransigence laid bare the hollowness of our relationship, which I had suspected since childhood. Sure, it hurt, but I had also grown tired of the charade. His unwillingness to acknowledge my pain, and his negligence as a parent, led me to understand that it wasn't my fault after all. I didn't deserve it. I didn't deserve to be left out in the cold like that, to be preyed upon. And I realized, with the drinking and aversion to talking about my pain, that I was following in his footsteps. I wasn't out of the woods yet, and I couldn't afford a therapist with temp jobs, student loans, and no insurance, but I was beginning to stand up for myself, in small ways no longer willing to deny the screams from within.

47

Some Cats Are Like That

Location: Greater Seattle Area & Las Vegas, NV
Age: 27-28

"You should do this for me," Mom said, sliding some paperwork my way. I rubbed my fingers over the table, noticing all the imprints in the wood from childhood homework. All the times I didn't listen well enough.

"What's this?" I asked. Mom nodded at the papers. I picked them up. It was from the A.A.R.P., one of those things people start to get in the mail when they're close to retirement age but not quite there yet. "Life insurance?" I chuckled in disbelief.

"I'm serious. It's a good rate."

The blinds along the sliding door rippled. A small, gray tabby cat, this one named Fritz, rubbed his side along them, then pawed at the door. I got up to open it for him. And he stood there, like a cat does, and waited a moment, contemplating if he truly wanted to walk around the yard or not.

"Mom, you're only 58," I said over my shoulder. I nudged Fritz with my foot. "I've got students loans. Someday, if I'm lucky, I'll have a mortgage, too. I don't want to spend the next 25 years paying this once a month." I closed the door. Fritz pawed at it again. I ignored him and returned to the table. "I mean, do you really think this is necessary?"

Mom stared at me.

"Are you okay, Mom? Is something going on?" I asked.

"I'm fine. This is just one of those things you're supposed to do. Your father left you nothing but his medals. My mother left me nothing, due to the Alzheimer's. It's not going to be the same when I go."

"Okay," I gave in. "You're sure you're okay though?" Mom had high cholesterol once when I was younger. She never ditched the booze, but she did convert to a diet high in oatmeal, blueberries, and green tea. Her job had her standing all day and the commute was brief. She belonged to a gym where she walked with her girlfriends. And she had finally found a nice man, her third husband. He was a huge improvement over those that came before. They bought a rambler together, so neither would have to walk up stairs when they got old.

"This is just something you need to do," she said.

"Okay. How much should I choose?" There were options for ten thousand, twenty-five thousand, fifty thousand, and one hundred thousand, with corresponding monthly rates.

"Whatever you think. Maybe ten?" She suggested.

"Well, I think I'll do twenty-five," I said, marking the selection on the paperwork.

"You'll be rich if I die."

"Oh come on. If you die anytime soon, most of the fucking money'll go to a shrink," I scoffed. Fritz meowed impatiently at the door. I got up again. This time he went out. I wondered why my ancestors found any use for such a species. "You know they'll look at your medical records, right? I mean, you've got to tell them everything when we fill this out or its for nothing." I sat back down.

"I'm not hiding anything," she said.

"It is a lot of money."

"You'll be rich if I die."

"Are you sure this is what you want to do?" I peered at her over the paperwork.

Mom made a sad smile.

I filled out the paperwork, then passed it back to her for the medical history part. I made a mental note to check that section before putting it in the mail.

We had dinner together that evening, then I headed home, forty minutes away. I worked in Bellevue and lived in Kirkland. Both are just east of Seattle, on the other side of Lake Washington.

I'd had "real" jobs for a few years now. The temp work was behind me. I worked at a university as an admissions counselor for a while, recruiting high schoolers to join the next freshmen class, until I became disillusioned over how that sausage got made. Now I was making a foray into Corporate America, working in an office with a desk and tons of incoming calls, helping ship chemicals all over the country. I hated the work immediately but told myself I had to stick it out. I was emotionally invested in being perceived as a success after all the time I spent stumbling through the Great Recession.

I had an unyielding desire to go on another adventure but told myself I couldn't. I needed to be serious now. I'd told myself that my entire life, it seemed. And the boy within screamed about running away and trying to have some fun before it was too late. I felt it already was. I was in my late twenties, after all, and had nothing to show for it. No wife and kids. No house. A big boy job in an office was the only part of my life that didn't make me feel like a failure.

So, I stayed. It was like a millennial version of *Office Space*, with the latest C.R.M. software and an open concept in lieu of cubicles. Typical wannabe techie. I stuck it out for six months, gaining weight, hating my life, until I just couldn't take it anymore.

Then, after yet another meeting about nothing, and a bonus check from the most patronizing boomer boss, I decided to quit and run away.

A friend from high school worked in Alaska for a tour company. I'd known others that had worked there too. The friend heard my complaints and offered me paid training in Las Vegas and a summer spent in Alaska and the Yukon Territory. I jumped at it. It was a huge pay cut and I'd be driving a tour bus all day, but it sounded exciting. Mom was the first one I told.

"Oh that sounds fun," she said on the phone that day.

"I am a little worried though. I wonder how it will affect my resume."

"I think employers would understand. A lot of them probably dream about going to Alaska too," she reassured me. "And you've never gone to Vegas, Zach. All those times your friends went, you just..."

"You don't think I'm doing something reckless?" I interrupted.

"As long as you stay away from the grizzlies, no."

"Thanks, Mom. I love you."

"I love you, too." We hung up the phone. I put in my two weeks' notice.

***

The next couple weeks were a breeze. All the little things that added up to misery at work no longer bothered me, as I could just ignore them, reminding myself that I was on my way out anyways. I packed up my belongings. I said goodbye to the friends I'd been renting from and headed to Mom's. The plan was to stay there for a night and then head out on an epic road trip to Las Vegas.

Mom and I had dinner together that evening, just the two of us, as her husband was on the night shift at that point. Baked chicken, mashed potatoes and gravy, and steamed broccoli and carrots. It was my favorite meal from childhood and Mom knew exactly how to make it.

"Are you excited?" she asked as we sat down to eat.

"Yeah, pretty excited," I cut off a piece of chicken, then dipped it in the potatoes and gravy. "I'm a little worried about L.A. traffic, but otherwise it'll be fine." I took a bite.

"What time you think you'll head out tomorrow?"

"Oh, I don't know. Maybe ten. I'm going to stop in central Oregon for the night, then I'm staying at a friend's place the next few nights down in Cali." Fritz hopped up on one of the vacant chairs and poked his head over the table. He looked hungry. "You haven't been feeding the pet from the table have you, Mom?" I teased. It was forbidden to do so when I was a kid.

"No. He's just watching. He's got wet food in the kitchen, don't ya Fritz?" she mothered at him. Fritz meowed. We both smiled. "I was just asking because we're doing pizza tomorrow at Rock Creek." She still worked as a lunch lady at the elementary school I attended as a child. I visited her at work whenever I was in town. And just like when I was a kid, she fed me for free.

"I can try. I just don't want to hit traffic ya know? I think leaving at ten is good." I shoveled more chicken and potatoes into my mouth.

"You really should come visit me tomorrow, Zach," Mom stated, firmly. She stared at me from across the table, her hands in her lap. She'd never invited me like that before. This didn't even sound like an invitation.

"Okay. Yeah, I can do that. I mean, I won't be seeing you for a while, right?"

"Right." Mom looked away, towards the living room, where Fritz now frolicked in front of the TV, wrestling with one of his toys. We finished eating, then watched a recorded episode of *Breaking Bad*.

***

I woke up at 11 the next morning and headed out after a quick shower. I parked at Rock Creek and got a visitor badge at the main office. Walking down the hallway after, I was struck by how tiny the school seemed to me now. It wasn't that long ago that a smaller version of me, confused and scared, wandered down that same hall, trying to stay in line with the rest of his class, excited to see his mother at lunch. I observed a class of 2nd graders, lunch bags in hand, in their little jackets, following their teacher to the cafeteria. It made me smile.

Mom and the other ladies were busy when I walked in. I sat at a small desk to wait for a lull in the line. Mom walked over a few minutes later with a large slice of cheese pizza. The cheese was white and appeared to be made of plastic.

"Want some milk or juice?" she asked, gesturing at the refrigerator.

"Nah, I'm alright. Thanks though." I started eating. Eventually, her work husband walked over and chatted with us for a while. He was a custodian and had been at the school longer than Mom. A kindhearted man.

"The next group will be here soon. You want to miss traffic too, right?" he asked.

"Yeah, I should get going. Thanks for letting me stay the night and everything," I said to Mom.

"I love you, Zach," Mom said. She hugged me and held on longer than usual. She always got emotional when I was going away for a while. Like when she dropped me off at the airport for my year-long teaching gig in Korea. Or when she dropped me off at my dorm freshmen year. This hug was desperate though. As she squeezed me, I felt her heartbeat. She put her face under my chin. *She's really worried about me.* I hugged her and rubbed her back.

"I'll be careful in L.A. Don't worry. I'm a safe driver," I said. She smiled. I walked away, then turned at the door. "Mom?" She turned around. "I love you, too. I'll see you when I'm on my way up to Alaska." I was going to drive back to Seattle after training in Las Vegas, then fly up to Alaska for the season. Mom nodded, then turned back to the pizza and eager children clamoring before her.

***

The road trip went exactly as planned. I stayed in Oregon one night and then made the long jaunt to Orange County. I stayed there a few days with one of my best friends, a guy I hadn't seen in a while. We went to a few beaches, reminisced, and ate some delicious food. Then I headed out to Vegas.

252

Unfortunately, the hotel we were housed in was far from The Strip, about an hour walk. I told myself it didn't matter though; I could make that walk. I really wanted the Vegas experience, to play some blackjack and have drinks by a pool, before watching the Bellagio fountain.

At check-in, I encountered two other dudes in town for training. One was an aspiring thespian sore from the Broncos losing the Super Bowl. The other, a redheaded wanderer who loved Franz Kafka, whom I'd never heard of before.

My room smelled of cigarette smoke, which made me think of my late father and the dingy apartments he occupied over the years. It made me sneeze. I considered complaining, but after checking out my new friends' accommodation, I realized this was par for the course.

The next few days ran together as my new friends and I, and all the other driver trainees, spent long hours in tour busses, taking turns driving around parking lots and side streets, learning about braking distance and how often to check your mirrors, trying to back around bright orange cones.

The bus I was on didn't seem to have air conditioning, or if it did, it was lousy. The armpits of my shirts were always stained by lunch and I'd change as soon as I got back to my room.

My new friends and I walked to The Strip one night when training let out early. The redhead tried to explain what "Kafkaesque" meant, but I'm not sure I got it. We snuck into a pool by walking right past a security guard to an elevator.

"You just have to act like you're a guest here," the redhead explained, as we sat down under a parasol. The chlorine mixed with the desert heat to form a unique aroma. I thought about jumping in the pool but didn't want a soggy walk home.

We had some drinks, then walked back to the hotel, promising each other we'd go back the next day to play some cards.

***

I was a tad hungover in the morning. Training was torture. The redhead and Broncos fan were both eager to go on another journey that evening, as they'd befriended a pretty brunette who wanted to go out. *I think I'd rather take a nap,* I thought as we walked back to the hotel. She seemed like a nice gal, but I was just too exhausted. In the end, my evening plans weren't really up to me.

The smell of stagnant cigarette smoke assaulted my nose as I walked into my room. The curtains were drawn but swayed as the air conditioning blew below the window. Flickers of late-day sunshine poked through them, animating small particles of dust dancing in the air.

I kicked off my shoes, my feet immediately feeling cold from the sweaty socks. I smelled my armpits, which had the masculine scent of some spicy wilderness mixed in with body odor. Then it occurred to me I hadn't checked my phone all day. The hangover and heat had distracted me from it. I pulled it out of my pocket.

There were three missed calls from Mom's husband. There was a voicemail, I assumed from him, and a text message asking that I call him as soon as I can. My legs trembled. I took a deep breath and sat down on a stiff, uneven bed, staring at my reflection in a mirror mounted to the wall. I made a sad smile, then called him back.

"I'm so sorry, Zach," he said as soon as he picked up. His voice was broken and high pitched.

"What happened?"

"I came home from work and Deb was face down along the ramp leading to the shed. Fritz was lying next to her. The E.M.T.s are still here but…" he paused for a moment. I heard a few labored gulps for air. Then his voice broke all over again. "I'm so sorry. She's dead. I did C.P.R. like 911 told me and the E.M.T.s tried when they got here, but she's gone. I'm so sorry." He sniffled.

My ears started ringing. It was like the sound of two empty wine glasses clinking together eternally. I kept looking at myself in the mirror, the day's fading light illuminating the right side of my face from the window, pieces of dust floating over my shoulder. My mouth was moving now, but I don't know what I said. I couldn't hear anything over the pitch of dread.

I know I got drunk alone that night. I know I called friends and family and my boss. I know I left the next day and drove back home, first over to California, then north on I-5 forever. But I don't remember any of it, aside from brief sequences of blurred vision and warm water on my face and my hands clutching a steering wheel.

48

Talk About It

Location: Alaska, Colorado, Greater Seattle Area
Age: 28-Present

I spent a month back home, filling out paperwork, talking to people, doing what I thought was my duty. Then I went to Alaska for the summer, then Colorado for the winter, then Alaska again. I went on a few road trips with new friends, most of whom were a bit broken inside like me. One of them killed himself. He was a veteran. Another one who fell through the cracks.

Eventually I made my way to Seattle and got another job in Corporate America. I hated it all over again, but it formed the springboard that got me a job that I thought would make me happy. I went to work in the tech sector, where I was paid more than twice as much as I'd ever made before. I had three different managers quit in my first month, but eventually one stuck around. She was a dream to work for. Even still, the work wore me down and I became depressed again.

Mom's estate got settled and the life insurance check cleared. My higher income combined with inheritance put me in a financial position to see a therapist, which I finally did at the behest of my friends. That was early fall, 2016.

Therapists are like dogs in some respects. They're friendly and have a keen sense of smell. Like dogs, they smell hidden things, and wander around your mind like they're looking for survivors after a flood. They can't save anyone on their own, but they can loudly point out where your attention needs to be and comfort you when you face the awful burden of not forgetting.

My raison d'etre for being in the therapist's office was grief from my mother's sudden passing. We talked about that, which invariably led to discussions about childhood, which led to my therapist asking me questions that I didn't want to hear out loud.

"You've mentioned your father being distant and negligent a few times now. Did you ever get hurt when you visited him?" he asked, sitting in a chair in a warm room that smelled vaguely of sage. I shifted in my seat on the beige couch in front of him. I glanced out the window, then pretended to look at the various potted plants scattered around his office. I betrayed myself and tried to play it off as something else.

"Yeah, there was this time when we were at the pool and Sarah jumped in with only one water wing on. She couldn't get her head above water and Papa didn't notice." I was the one that noticed and saved her from drowning.

"Mmmhmmm," he said. He looked at me and there was a softness in his eyes. A few bricks slipped and fell down the wall I'd built. I thought about James.

"I mean, he had a friend that came by sometimes, to ya know, help out with the childcare," I mentioned.

"Did this friend of his ever hurt you?" he asked. I could tell from the look on his face that he already knew the answer. He'd

257

been doing this for 30 years after all. *What do I have to lose?* A nervous laugh escaped from my mouth.

"Yeah, he did. He molested me." I looked at the floor.

"There's nothing to be ashamed of, Zach. This is a very common experience. A lot of boys and girls go through this. Sexual predators often target families experiencing chaos, like in the aftermath of a divorce. None of that was your fault."

It made me want to cry, but the thought of that made me feel embarrassed, so I flexed my jaw and we sat in silence for a few moments. Nonetheless, that was a breakthrough for me. I'd never stated it explicitly like that, even with James a decade before.

About the Author

Zach Neuhaus was born in Seattle but raised in Maple Valley, Washington. He has a bachelor's degree in Political Science from Western Washington University. He accidentally qualified himself to work in HR in Corporate America, where he remains. Zach still sees a shrink. *Big Boy* is his first book.